DATE DUE

JY 10 '97			

PRINTED IN U.S.A.

D0852134

Great Meals in Minutes was created by Rebus, Inc.
and published by Time-Life Books.

Rebus, Inc.

Publisher: Rodney Friedman
Editorial Director: Shirley Tomkievicz

Editor: Marya Dalrymple
Art Director: Ronald Gross
Managing Editor: Brenda Goldberg
Senior Editor: Charles Blackwell
Food Editor and Food Stylist: Grace Young
Photographer: Steven Mays
Prop Stylist: Cathryn Schwing
Staff Writer: Alexandra Greeley
Associate Editor: Bonnie J. Slotnick
Editorial Assistant: Ned Miller
Assistant Food Stylist: Karen Hatt
Photography Assistant: Lars Klove
Recipe Tester: Gina Palombi Barclay
Production Assistant: Lisa Young

For information about any Time-Life book, please write:
Reader Information
Time-Life Books
541 North Fairbanks Court
Chicago, Illinois 60611
Library of Congress Cataloging in Publication Data
Mediterranean menus.
   (Great meals in minutes)
   Includes index.
   1. Cookery, Mediterranean. 2. Menus.
I. Time-Life Books. II. Series.
TX725.M35M44   1985   642′.1   85-8498
ISBN 0-86706-294-0 (lib. bdg.)
ISBN 0-86706-293-2 (retail ed.)

Time-Life Books Inc.
is a wholly owned subsidiary of

Time Incorporated

Founder: Henry R. Luce 1898–1967

Editor-in-Chief: Henry Anatole Grunwald
President: J. Richard Munro
Chairman of the Board: Ralph P. Davidson
Corporate Editor: Jason McManus
Group Vice President, Books: Reginald K. Brack Jr.
Vice President, Books: George Artandi

Time-Life Books Inc.

Editor: George Constable
Executive Editor: George Daniels
Editorial General Manager: Neal Goff
Director of Design: Louis Klein
Editorial Board: Dale M. Brown, Roberta Conlan, Ellen Phillips, Gerry Schremp, Gerald Simons, Rosalind Stubenberg, Kit van Tulleken, Henry Woodhead
Director of Research: Phyllis K. Wise
Director of Photography: John Conrad Weiser

President: William J. Henry
Senior Vice President: Christopher T. Linen
Vice Presidents: Stephen L. Bair, Robert A. Ellis, John M. Fahey Jr., Juanita T. James, James L. Mercer, Joanne A. Pello, Paul R. Stewart, Christian Strasser

Editorial Operations
Design: Ellen Robling (assistant director)
Copy Room: Diane Ullius
Editorial Operations: Caroline A. Boubin (manager)
Production: Celia Beattie
Quality Control: James J. Cox (director), Sally Collins
Library: Louise D. Forstall

SERIES CONSULTANT
Margaret E. Happel is the author of *Ladies' Home Journal Adventures in Cooking*, *Ladies' Home Journal Handbook of Holiday Cuisine*, and other best-selling cookbooks, as well as the translator and adapter of Rebecca Hsu Hiu Min's *Delights of Chinese Cooking*. A food consultant based in New York City, she has been director of the food department of *Good Housekeeping* and editor of *American Home* magazine.

WINE CONSULTANT
Tom Maresca combines a full-time career teaching English literature with writing about and consuming fine wines. He is the author of *Mastering Wine a Taste at a Time*.

Cover: Rowena Hubbard's Moroccan *couscous* with *harissa* sauce, and orange and olive salad. See pages 46–49.

Great Meals
IN MINUTES

MEDITERRANEAN MENUS

TIME
LIFE
BOOKS

TIME-LIFE BOOKS, ALEXANDRIA, VIRGINIA

Contents

Meet the Cooks

SUSAN DeREGE

Canadian-born Susan DeRege is married to the son of an Italian diplomat. She spends summers at their family home in Piedmont and travels throughout Italy gathering unusual and authentic recipes. She teaches Italian cooking at the New School Culinary Arts Program in New York City and at Kings Cookingstudio in Short Hills, New Jersey.

MARIA AND GUY REUGE

Maria and Guy Reuge live on Long Island, New York, and are the owners of Mirabelle, a restaurant specializing in country French cooking with regional American overtones. A native of Orleans, France, Guy Reuge is a classically trained chef and is responsible for all of the cooking at their restaurant. Maria Reuge, who grew up in Virginia, was formerly an editor at *Gourmet* and now develops recipes with her husband.

STEVIE BASS

Born and raised in Connecticut, Stevie Bass studied art and design as well as food and nutrition in college, and she uses this training in her work as a recipe developer and food stylist. Now living in San Francisco, she runs her own consulting firm, Food Concepts, which works with advertising and public relations agencies, photographers, filmmakers, and food companies in the Bay Area.

ROWENA M. HUBBARD

Rowena Hubbard, a home economist and nutritionist, has worked as a dietitian and director of consumer affairs for several corporations and has written hundreds of recipe leaflets and cookbooks, including *California Cooks*. She is managing partner of Anderson, Miller & Hubbard, food publicists in San Francisco.

SILVANA LA ROCCA

The daughter of an Italian diplomat, Silvana La Rocca was born and raised in the Abruzzo region of Italy. She has also lived in Rome and has traveled extensively in Europe and South America. Although she holds a Master's Degree in international law, Silvana La Rocca prefers to cook for a living. She lives in Berkeley, California, where she operates Made to Order, a delicatessen, take-out, and catering business.

GEORGIA DOWNARD

Georgia Downard holds three different diplomas from L'Ecole de Cuisine La Varenne in Paris. She cooked at Claude's, a French restaurant in New York City, and has served as a food editor at *Gourmet*. She now freelances as a food stylist and recipe developer, and is working on several cookbooks. She is a member of the New York Women's Culinary Alliance.

JEAN ANDERSON

A native of Raleigh, North Carolina, Jean Anderson first cooked at the age of five, beginning a lifelong interest in food. After earning a B.S. in food and nutrition at Cornell University and a graduate degree in journalism at Columbia University, she became a food editor and later managing editor of *Ladies' Home Journal*. Now a freelance photojournalist, she writes regularly for many major magazines and is the author of twelve cookbooks.

JOYCE GOLDSTEIN

San Franciscan Joyce Goldstein began her food career in 1965 teaching informal cooking classes. After founding the California Street Cooking School, she worked as head chef, recipe planner, and manager at the Chez Panisse Café in Berkeley. Today she cooks at her own restaurant, Square One, which features a menu focusing on Mediterranean, Latin American, and American foods.

DENNIS GILBERT

After graduate school, Dennis Gilbert decided to combine two careers: cooking and writing. He apprenticed with a chef in Maine and trained in restaurants specializing in classical and regional French cooking. He is now *chef de cuisine* at the Vinyard Restaurant in Portland, Maine, and also teaches English at the University of Southern Maine. His short stories have appeared in numerous publications.

Mediterranean Menus in Minutes
GREAT MEALS FOR FOUR IN AN HOUR OR LESS

Since antiquity, the Mediterranean has engendered both history and myth. Alexander the Great, King Minos, Ulysses, Cleopatra, and Hannibal are names that conjure up the mystery and the magic of a region that spans three continents and some sixteen countries, including Spain, Portugal, France, Italy, Greece, Turkey, Egypt, and Morocco. These contiguous lands, seemingly saturated in perpetual light and fragrance, either encircle or are influenced by the 500-mile-wide, 2,500-mile-long Mediterranean Sea.

The Mediterranean is an aquatic highway that culturally and geographically links the disparate countries that border it. Moreover, the constant crisscrossing of the sea by traders who settled and resettled along its shores has created a common culinary idiom—the widespread use of olives and olive oil, wild herbs and exotic spices, garlic, honey, nuts, and orange and rose waters. The sea also affects the region's climate (hot and dry in summer and chilly and damp in winter) and its soil and vegetation; crops such as wheat, olives, grapes, and rice have been grown since ancient times in nearly all of the Mediterranean countries. In addition, some 400 species of fish and shellfish are found in its waters.

Still, Mediterranean cooking defies easy definition. It is at once simple and elaborate, gentle and fiery, homogeneous and diverse. Grilled meats and vegetables subtly flavored with lemon and olive oil are as Mediterranean in character as are the more aromatic fish stews or the endless varieties of *couscous* (meat and vegetables served with steamed grains).

To a great extent, the seasons dictate the menu: In spring, markets overflow with asparagus, lettuce, cherries, strawberries, and figs; in summer, with eggplant, zucchini, peppers, tomatoes, melons, plums, and lemons; in fall, with mushrooms, artichokes, fennel, grapes, and quinces; and in winter, with leeks, turnips, carrots, oranges, and grapefruits. These ingredients are ubiquitous throughout the Mediterranean; in fact, a Greek cook would feel right at home shopping in a Moroccan market.

Any culinary differences that do arise generally reflect religious or ethnic choices. For instance, the Spaniards, French, Italians, and Greeks all eat pork with gusto, but their Israeli and Arab neighbors consider pork taboo. On the other hand, lamb—spitted whole or cubed for stews or shish kabobs—is a Greek, Turkish, and Middle Eastern staple but is less favored by other Mediterranean cooks. Despite such differences, Mediterraneans are united by their passion for fine foods lovingly prepared and served with an exuberance and sensuousness found nowhere else in the world.

On the following pages, ten of America's most talented cooks present 27 complete menus with recipes that derive from Mediterranean cuisine. Each menu, which serves four people, can be prepared in an hour or less, and all have been adapted to American kitchens; yet each recipe retains the spirit of the Mediterranean, using fresh produce and seafood and good cuts of meat. Additional ingredients (vinegars, spices, herbs, and so on) are all of high quality and are widely available in supermarkets or occasionally in specialty food stores.

The cooks and the kitchen staff have meticulously planned and tested the meals for appearance as well as for taste, as the accompanying photographs show: The vegetables are brilliant and fresh, the visual combinations appetizing. The table settings feature bright colors, simple flower arrangements, and attractive but not necessarily expensive serving dishes.

For each menu, the Editors, with advice from the cooks, suggest wines and other beverages. And there are suggestions for the use of leftovers and for complementary dishes and desserts. On each menu page, you will find a number of tips, from an easy method for shelling and deveining shrimp to advice for selecting the freshest eggplants.

BEFORE YOU START
Great Meals in Minutes is designed for efficiency and ease. This book will work best for you if you follow these suggestions:

1. Refresh your memory with the few simple cooking techniques on the following pages. They will quickly become second nature and will help you to produce professional-quality meals in minutes.

2. Read the menus before you shop. Each lists the ingredients you will need, in the order that you would expect to shop for them. Many items will already be on your pantry shelf.

Awaiting preparation, opposite, the ingredients that form the foundation of Mediterranean cooking. Clockwise from top left: fish and shellfish, bulgur and couscous, extra-virgin olive oil, lamb and fresh mint, olives, cinnamon and coffee, saffron and bay leaves, fresh and dried fruits, nuts, ginger, and perfectly ripe melons.

Cooking at high temperatures will be less dangerous if you follow a few simple tips:

▶ Water added to hot fat will always cause spattering. If possible, pat foods dry with a cloth or paper towel before you add them to the hot oil.

▶ Place food gently into any pan containing hot fat, or the fat will spatter.

▶ If you are boiling or steaming some foods while sautéing others, place the pots on the stove top far enough apart so that the water is unlikely to splash into the hot fat.

▶ Turn pot handles inward, so that you do not accidentally knock over a pot containing hot foods or liquids.

▶ Remember that alcohol—wine, brandy, or spirits—may catch fire when you add it to a very hot pan. If this happens, step back for your own protection and quickly cover the pan with a lid. The fire will instantly subside, and the food will not be spoiled.

▶ Keep pot holders and mitts close enough to be handy while cooking, but *never* hang them over the burners or lay them on the stove top.

---

3. Check the equipment list on page 14. Good sharp knives and pots and pans of the right shape and material are essential for making great meals in minutes. This may be the time to buy a few things. The right equipment can turn cooking from a necessity into a creative experience.

4. Set out everything you will need before you start to cook: The lists at the beginning of each menu tell just what is required. To save effort, always keep your ingredients in the same place so you can reach for them instinctively.

5. Remove meat, fish, and eggs from the refrigerator early enough for them to reach room temperature.

6. Follow the start-to-finish steps for each menu. That way, you can be sure of having the entire meal ready to serve in an hour.

A GASTRONOMIC TOUR OF THE MEDITERRANEAN
The following brief tour of the Mediterranean moves clockwise around the sea, beginning with the Iberian Peninsula and ending with the North African country of Morocco. It highlights the regions and countries that have inspired the recipes in this volume.

The Iberian Peninsula
Bounded by the Atlantic Ocean and the Mediterranean, the Iberian Peninsula includes the countries of Portugal and Spain. On the whole, Iberian food is rustic and powerful. Iberian cooks are particularly concerned with artfully combining fresh ingredients to preserve their individual flavors. Even though they share a common larder of olive oil, olives, garlic, parsley, fresh fish and shellfish, and red and green peppers, as well as many of the same cooking methods, Spanish and Portuguese dishes rarely taste alike. The Portuguese cook with cream and butter, and love to season dishes heavily (the influence of their former colonies of Angola, Mozambique, Goa, and Brazil). The Spaniards, on the other hand, use little butter and only minimal spicing. Contrary to popular belief, Spanish food is not fiery.

The cooking of southern Spain, especially that of the sunny and populous region of Andalusia (the last Moorish stronghold), is generally light and delicate. Andalusians rarely serve roasts, rich stews, or heavy sauces; instead, they are famous for their quick-fried fish, *gazpacho*

(chilled puréed vegetable soup), and *sangría* (a fruity red wine punch). Dennis Gilbert offers a typical Andalusian menu featuring fried haddock on page 102.

Mountainous Catalonia, which includes the Costa Brava, or "rugged coast," lies to the northeast of Andalusia. Here the climate is cooler, so cooks tend to prepare heartier dishes, including their noted *zarzuelas*, or seafood stews. Grapes grow abundantly on Catalonia's hillsides, and many of Spain's wines come from this region. On page 96, Dennis Gilbert suggests a typical Catalonian meal of roast baby chickens with sausage and cabbage.

Southern France
With their coastlines bordering the warm Mediterranean waters, the neighboring regions of Languedoc and Provence are blessed with an abundance of seafood. The cooks here are proud of their seafood stews, in particular *bourride*, made with a variety of white fish and mixed with *aïoli* (garlic mayonnaise), and *bouillabaisse*, which traditionally includes Mediterranean rockfish and is found in its true form only in and around Marseilles. In these regions, too, the overwhelming fragrances of lavender, mint, and garlic fill the fresh sea air, and open-air markets are filled with pyramids of carefully stacked produce.

Although southern French cooking is for the most part simple and practical, traces of the more exotic North African cooking still linger—vestiges of the days when the French held colonies in that part of the world. Today the famous North African *couscous* remains a popular Provençal dish. On pages 28 and 33, Maria and Guy Reuge offer two Provençal dinners, one featuring sautéed monkfish with fresh tomato sauce and the other a fish stew seasoned with saffron. Their third menu of mussels stuffed with herbed almond butter is typical of Languedoc.

Italy
The crescent-shaped region called Liguria on the Gulf of Genoa is better known to the rest of the world as the Italian Riviera. Its principal port, Genoa, influences the cooking of the entire region, with its focus on freshly caught seafood combined with aromatic herbs grown on

the nearby hillsides. Basil, the best known of the Genoese herbs, can be seen growing everywhere—in flower pots and wild in the countryside. Basil is the basis for *pesto Genovese*, a cheese, garlic, and herb paste often served in soups or spooned over pasta. Minestrone, a stew-like vegetable soup made with pasta, is another specialty of this region—the Genoese claim to have invented it, along with ravioli. Susan DeRege serves three Genoese meals, all of which feature seafood and fresh basil in one guise or another.

Abruzzo, a mountainous region with its coastline on the eastern shores of Italy, has always been a farming area. Here, the cooking is based on local produce. Goats and sheep graze on the mountain slopes and provide the milk for Abruzzo's cheeses, such as creamy *scamorza* and spicy *caciocavallo di pescocostanzo*, and pigs and lambs are raised for their meat. Along the coast, fish dishes abound, often prepared with the white wine vinegar for which the region is known. Abruzzese cooks frequently spark their dishes with hot peppers. Silvana La Rocca was born and raised in Abruzzo. Her fresh salmon steaks with green sauce, page 56, *penne* (quill-shaped pasta) with seafood, page 59, and rabbit with hot pepper flakes, page 62, are adaptations of recipes popular in this region.

Greece

The land of Greece, encompassing the mainland peninsula (which juts 500 miles into the Mediterranean) and its hundreds of islands, is home to an ancient and venerable cuisine. Although nearly 400 years of Turkish rule left its mark on Greek cooking, local cooks still pride themselves on their own versions of cinnamon-scented casseroles, roast lamb dishes with yogurt, and honey-soaked nut-filled pastries. Fresh seafood is a prominent part of the Greek diet, and sheep and pigs are raised on the rocky, rugged terrain. Farmers grow wheat and other grains, and numerous vegetables thrive in the temperate climate. Still, it is the liberal use of olive oil that unites Greek cooks. Greek mythology describes how the Olympian goddess Athena brought the olive tree to Greece, and since those ancient days, the olive and its oil have figured prominently in every aspect of Greek life and cooking. On pages 41 and 44, Stevie Bass offers two popular Greek dishes using olive oil: *moussaka*, a rich eggplant casserole, and broiled lamb kabobs.

Turkey

Situated on the eastern tip of the Mediterranean Sea, Turkey is the culinary buffer zone between the neighboring Arab world and the Balkan countries of Eastern Europe. Consequently, Turkish cooking is an amalgam of gently flavored meat stews and plain grilled fish and the more elaborate spicing that characterizes Middle Eastern foods. Having arisen from nomadic and peasant origins, Turkish cooking is still a cuisine of easily portable foods and one-dish meals; but today these foods are as at home on banquet tables as they once were on the road or in the fields. Fine examples of Turkish dishes are shish kabobs, meat-stuffed tomatoes and peppers, and spicy casseroles

---

Making Chicken Stock

Although canned chicken broth or stock is all right for emergencies, homemade chicken stock has a rich flavor that is hard to match. Moreover, the commercial broths—particularly the canned ones—are likely to be oversalted.

To make your own stock, save chicken parts as they accumulate and put them in a bag in the freezer; then have a rainy-day stock-making session using the recipe below. The skin from a yellow onion will add color; the optional veal bone will add extra flavor and richness.

3 pounds bony chicken parts, such as wings, back, and neck
1 veal knuckle (optional)
3 quarts cold water
1 unpeeled yellow onion, stuck with two cloves
2 stalks celery with leaves, cut in two
12 crushed peppercorns
2 carrots, scraped and cut into 2-inch lengths
4 sprigs parsley
1 bay leaf
1 tablespoon fresh thyme, or 1 teaspoon dried
Salt (optional)

1. Wash chicken parts and veal knuckle (if you are using it) and drain. Place in large soup kettle or stockpot (any big pot) with the remaining ingredients—except salt. Cover pot and bring to a boil over moderate heat.

2. Lower heat and simmer stock, partly covered, 2 to 3 hours. Skim foam and scum from top of stock several times. Add salt to taste after stock has cooked 1 hour.

3. Strain stock through fine sieve placed over large bowl. Discard solids. Let stock cool uncovered (this will speed cooling process). When completely cool, refrigerate. Fat will rise and congeal conveniently at top. You may skim it off and discard it or leave it as a protective covering until ready to use.

Yield: About 10 cups

---

often filled with lamb and eggplant. Freshly made yogurt is served at nearly every meal. Turks always conclude their dinners with a sweet pastry, such as the famous *baklava*, layered with chopped nuts and sugar syrup, and with tiny cups of thick, potent coffee. On pages 88–90, Joyce Goldstein serves a Turkish meal of spinach soup with yogurt and dill, marinated broiled chicken, and pilaf studded with currants and pistachios.

Middle East

Known as the cradle of civilization, the Middle East (which includes Egypt, Iraq, Syria, Jordan, Israel, and Lebanon) was probably the cradle of *haute cuisine* as well. Recently deciphered stone tablets reveal that 4,000 years ago Mesopotamian master chefs developed a repertoire that included 100 kinds of soup, 18 different cheeses, and 300 varieties of bread. Today, Middle Eastern cooks continue to amplify this exotic cuisine, which, unlike that of other Mediterranean countries, uses *samna* (a clarified butter often made from buffalo's milk) rather than olive or vegetable oil for cooking. Certain other ingredients are more prevalent as well, including chickpeas, grape leaves (for wrapping savory stuffings), sesame seeds, mint, walnuts, and pomegranates. On pages 74–83, Jean Anderson presents Middle Eastern menus featuring swordfish kabobs, *falafel* (ground chickpeas) with *tahini* (a sauce made from ground sesame seeds), and *tabbouleh* salad (here made with bulgur, chopped onion, tomatoes, and mint).

Morocco

Located in northwest Africa, with the Atlantic and the Mediterranean at its shores, the kingdom of Morocco has a lavish cuisine inherited from the Arabs, French, Spanish, and Portuguese who traded and settled there. From the ports of Tangier and Casablanca along its coasts to Fez and Marrakesh farther inland, spicy breads, innumerable varieties of *couscous* (the pride of Morocco), meats stewed with fruits, and whole fish stuffed with nuts and vegetables—all fragrant with such spices as cinnamon, ginger, cumin, and saffron—are the hallmarks of Morocco's cuisine. On pages 46–53, Rowena Hubbard explores Moroccan cooking in three menus that include *couscous*

moistened with *harissa* (hot pepper sauce), lamb with apricots, and spicy chicken served with cracked-wheat pilaf.

GENERAL COOKING TECHNIQUES
Sautéing

Sautéing is a form of quick frying with no cover on the pan. In French, *sauter* means "to jump," which is what vegetables or small pieces of food do when you shake the sauté pan. The purpose is to brown the food lightly and seal in the juices, sometimes before further cooking. This technique has three critical elements: the right pan, the proper temperature, and dry food.

The sauté pan: A proper sauté pan is 10 to 12 inches in diameter and has 2- to 3-inch straight sides that allow you to turn the food and still keep the fat from spattering. It has a heavy bottom that can be moved back and forth easily across a burner.

The best material (and the most expensive) for a sauté pan is tin-lined copper, because it is a superior heat conductor. Heavy-gauge aluminum works well but will discolor acidic food like tomatoes. Therefore, you should not

Yogurt

Yogurt is a semi-solid milk fermented by the action of beneficial bacterial cultures. Often hailed as a wonder food that promotes longevity and immunizes against infection, yogurt in fact has about the same nutritional value as milk but is more digestible.

Various legends attribute the discovery of yogurt to the work of gods and angels in India or Persia. But most probably it is the cooks of the ancient Middle East to whom the credit is due. Today yogurt is popular worldwide, but in the Middle East, Greece, Turkey, and North Africa it has been an indispensable food for centuries, served plain as a sauce for meats and vegetables, stirred into soups, sweetened for desserts, and diluted with water as a refreshing beverage.

Although in the United States both plain and sweetened yogurts are available in supermarkets and health food stores, homemade yogurt far surpasses these commercial varieties. It is easy and economical to make and requires no special equipment or skills. All you need is a nonaluminum saucepan or kettle, a thermometer to test the temperature of the heated milk, and clean glass containers, such as canning jars, for incubating it. Or, if you prefer, you can purchase a yogurt maker for incubating the milk.

A good-quality starter that will ferment the milk properly is essential to the yogurt-making process. Use plain commercial yogurt (or yogurt saved from a prior batch of homemade) or dried yogurt culture, available at health food stores. Allow 2 tablespoons of fresh yogurt or 1 tablespoon of dried culture for each quart of milk. The milk can be whole, part condensed and part whole, or skimmed. If you use skimmed milk, add ½ to 1 cup of nonfat dry milk to each quart to give the yogurt the proper texture.

Heat the milk in a large heavy-gauge nonaluminum saucepan to 115 degrees (or if you are using a yogurt maker, follow the manufacturer's directions.) As soon as the milk reaches

115 degrees, remove it from the heat and add the starter. (For a sweetened yogurt, stir in sweetener, and vanilla extract if desired, at this point.) Pour the mixture into the storage containers and cover tightly with lids or plastic wrap.

To insulate the containers, wrap them in a bath towel or blanket. Place the wrapped containers in a warm place, such as an oven warmed by a pilot light or on a heating pad set at low. Be sure the containers are out of direct sunlight and that the temperature of the yogurt does not go above 120 degrees (which will destroy the good bacteria) or below 90 degrees (at which point the bacteria cease to be active). Leave the yogurt undisturbed for four or more hours, depending on the container size. When the yogurt is thick enough to hold its shape in a spoon, remove the containers from the heat source and refrigerate them for at least three hours before serving. The yogurt will continue to thicken as it chills.

Covered tightly, homemade yogurt will keep for 1 to 2 weeks in the refrigerator. Remember, because yogurt contains living organisms, the batches may vary in taste and texture from time to time. For the best and most consistent results, be sure that the milk and the starter are fresh, the containers clean, and that you allow sufficient time for incubation.

The following recipe is for *ayran*, a plain but refreshing Turkish yogurt drink. You can enhance the mixture by adding nutmeg, ginger, or cinnamon to taste, or chopped fresh herbs such as parsley, mint, or dill.

1 pint plain yogurt
1 cup ice water
Pinch of salt

Combine all ingredients in the container of a blender or food processor and process until foamy. Serve immediately.

use aluminum if acidic food is to be cooked for more than 20 minutes after the initial browning. Another option is to select a heavy-duty sauté pan made of strong, heat-conducting aluminum alloys. This type of professional cookware is smooth and stick resistant.

Use a sauté pan large enough to hold the food without crowding, or sauté in two batches. The heat of the fat and the air spaces around and between the pieces facilitate browning.

Many recipes call for sautéing first, then lowering the heat and cooking the food, covered, for an additional 10 to 20 minutes. Be sure you buy a sauté pan with a tight-fitting cover. Make certain the handle is long and is comfortable to hold. Use a wooden spatula or tongs to keep food moving in the pan as you shake it over the burner. If the food sticks, as it occasionally will, a metal spatula will loosen it best. Turn the food so that all surfaces come into contact with the hot fat.

Never immerse the hot pan in cold water because this will warp the metal. Allow the pan to cool slightly, then add water and let it sit until you are ready to wash it.

The fat: Half butter and half vegetable or peanut oil is perfect for most sautéing: It heats to high temperatures without burning, yet gives a rich butter flavor. For cooking, unsalted butter tastes best and adds no extra salt.

Some sautéing recipes in this book call for olive oil, which imparts a delicious and distinctive flavor of its own and is less sensitive than butter to high heat. Nevertheless, even the finest olive oil has some residue of fruit pulp, which will occasionally scorch. Watch carefully when you sauté in olive oil; discard any scorched oil and start with fresh, if necessary.

To sauté properly, heat the fat until it is hot but not smoking. When you see small bubbles on top of the fat, lower the heat because the fat is on the verge of smoking. When using butter and oil together, add butter to the hot oil. After the foam from the melting butter subsides, you are ready to sauté. If the temperature of the fat is just right, the food will sizzle when you put it in the pan. Jean Anderson sautés chicken breasts, page 82.

Blanching

Also called parboiling, blanching is an invaluable technique. Immerse whole or cut vegetables or other foods for a few minutes in boiling water, then refresh them, that is, plunge them into cold water to stop their cooking and set their colors. Blanching softens or tenderizes dense or crisp vegetables, often as a preliminary to further cooking by another method, such as stir frying. Silvana La Rocca blanches onions, page 63.

Steaming

Steaming is a fast and nutritious way to cook vegetables and other food. Bring water to a boil in a saucepan. Place the food in a steamer or on a rack over the liquid and cover the pan, periodically checking the water level. Keeping the food above the liquid preserves vitamins and minerals often lost in other methods of cooking. Stevie Bass steams green beans, page 42.

Deglazing

Deglazing is an easy way to create a sauce for sautéed, braised, or roasted food. To deglaze a pan, pour off all but 1 or 2 tablespoons of the fat in which the food has been cooked. Add liquid—water, wine, or stock—and reduce the sauce over medium heat, using a wooden spoon to scrape up the concentrated juices and brown bits of food clinging to the bottom of the pan. Maria and Guy Reuge use this technique in preparing pork chops with anchovy sauce, page 32.

Poaching

You poach meat, fish, chicken, fruit, and eggs in very hot liquid in a pan on top of the stove. You can use water or, better still, beef, chicken, or fish stock, or a combination of stock and white wine, or even cream as the poaching liquid. Joyce Goldstein poaches eggs in Menu 3, page 92.

Roasting and Baking

Roasting is a dry-heat process, usually used for large cuts of meat and poultry, that cooks the food by exposing it to heated air in an oven or, perhaps, a covered barbecue. For more even circulation of heat, the food should be placed in a shallow pan or on a rack in a pan. For greater moisture retention, baste the food with its own juices, fat, or a flavorful marinade. Dennis Gilbert roasts baby chickens, page 96.

Baking applies to the dry-heat cooking of foods such as casseroles; small cuts of meat, fish, and poultry; vegetables; and, of course, breads and pastries. Some foods are baked tightly covered to retain their juices and flavors; others, such as breads, cakes, and cookies, are baked in open pans to release moisture. After braising red snapper, Susan DeRege bakes it, page 18.

Broiling and Grilling

These are two relatively fast ways to cook meat, poultry, and fish, giving food a crisp exterior while leaving the inside juicy. Whether broiling or grilling, brush the food with melted fat, a sauce, or marinade before you cook. This adds flavor and moisture.

In broiling, the food cooks directly under the heat source. In grilling, the food cooks either directly over an open fire or on a well-seasoned griddle placed directly over a burner. Susan DeRege grills tuna steaks, page 22.

Braising

Braising is simmering meats or vegetables in a relatively small amount of liquid, usually for a long period of time. Sometimes the food is browned or parboiled before braising. You may wish to flavor the braising liquid with herbs, spices, and aromatic vegetables, or use wine, stock, or tomato sauce as a medium. Georgia Downard braises duck with eggplant, page 70.

Pan Frying

The food cooks, uncovered, in a small amount of fat, which has been preheated in a heavy skillet. Pan frying is a quick cooking method suitable for thin-cut chops, steaks, and other foods. Dennis Gilbert pan fries haddock steaks, page 102.

Pantry (for this volume)

A well-stocked, properly organized pantry is essential for preparing great meals in the shortest time possible. Whether your pantry consists of a small refrigerator and two or three shelves over the sink, or a large freezer, refrigerator, and entire room just off the kitchen, you must protect staples from heat and light.

In maintaining your pantry, follow these rules:

1. Store staples by kind and date. Canned goods, canisters, and spices need a separate shelf, or a separate spot on a shelf. Date all staples—shelved, refrigerated, or frozen—by writing the date directly on the package or on a bit of masking tape. Then put the oldest ones in front to be sure you use them first.

2. Store flour, sugar, and other dry ingredients in canisters or jars with tight lids. Glass and clear plastic allow you to see at a glance how much remains.

3. Keep a running grocery list so that you can note when a staple is half gone, and be sure to stock up.

ON THE SHELF:

Anchovies
Anchovy fillets, both flat and rolled, come oil-packed, in tins.

Capers
Capers are usually packed in vinegar and less frequently in salt. If you use the latter, you should rinse them under cold water before using them.

Chickpeas
Also called *garbanzos* or *ceci*. Canned chickpeas are used for the recipes in this volume.

Dried fruits
apricots
raisins

Flour
all-purpose, bleached or unbleached

Garlic
Store in a cool, dry, well-ventilated place. Garlic powder and garlic salt are not adequate substitutes for fresh garlic.

Herbs and spices
The flavor of fresh herbs is much better than that of dried. Fresh herbs should be refrigerated and used as soon as possible. The following herbs are perfectly acceptable dried, but buy in small amounts, store airtight in dry area away from heat and light, and use as quickly as possible. In measuring herbs, remember that one part dried will equal three parts fresh. Crushing dried herbs brings out their flavor: Use a mortar and pestle or sandwich the herbs between 2 sheets of waxed paper and crush with a rolling pin.
Note: Dried chives and parsley should not be on your shelf, since they have little or no flavor; frozen chives are acceptable. Buy whole spices rather than ground, as they keep their flavor much longer. Grind spices at home and store as directed for herbs.

basil
bay leaves
Cayenne pepper
cinnamon
coriander
cumin
fennel seeds
ginger
marjoram
mint
nutmeg, whole and ground
oregano
paprika
pepper
> *black peppercorns*
> These are unripe peppercorns dried in their husks. Grind with a pepper mill for each use.
> *white peppercorns*
> These are the same as the black variety, but are picked ripe and husked. Use them in pale sauces when black pepper specks would spoil the appearance.
red pepper flakes (also called crushed red pepper)
rosemary

saffron
> Made from the dried stigmas of a species of crocus, this spice—the most costly of all seasonings—adds both color and flavor. Available powdered or in threads. Use sparingly.
salt
> Use coarse salt—commonly available as kosher or sea—for its superior flavor, texture, and purity. Kosher salt and sea salt are less salty than table salt. Substitute in the following proportions: three-quarters teaspoon table salt equals just under one teaspoon kosher or sea salt.
savory
tarragon
thyme

Honey

Nuts, whole, chopped or slivered
almonds
pine nuts (pignoli)
walnuts

Oils
corn, safflower, or vegetable
> Because these neutral-tasting oils have high smoking points, they are good for high-heat sautéing.
olive oil
> Olive oil ranges in color from pale yellow to dark green and in taste from mild and delicate to rich and fruity. Different olive oils can be used for different purposes: for example, stronger ones for cooking, lighter ones for salads. The finest-quality olive oil is labeled extra-virgin or virgin.

Olives
green olives
Kalamata olives
> Dark purple almond-shaped Greek olives that have been brine cured and packed in vinegar.
oil-cured black olives

Onions
Store all dry-skinned onions in a cool, dry, well-ventilated place.
red or Italian onions
> Zesty tasting and generally eaten raw. The perfect salad onion.
shallots
> The most subtle member of the onion family, the shallot has a delicate garlic flavor.
white onions
> Also called boiling onions, these small onions are almost always cooked and served whole.
yellow onions
> All-purpose cooking onions, strong in taste.

Pimientos

Potatoes, boiling and baking
"New" potatoes are not a particular kind of potato, but any potato that has not been stored.

Rice
long-grain white rice
> Slender grains, much longer than they are wide, that become light and fluffy when cooked and are best

for general use.

Stock, chicken

For maximum flavor and quality, your own stock is best (see recipe page 9), but canned stock, or broth, is adequate for most recipes and convenient to have on hand.

Sugar

granulated sugar

Tomatoes

Italian plum tomatoes

Canned plum tomatoes (preferably imported) are an acceptable substitute for fresh.

tomato paste

Sometimes available in tubes, which can be refrigerated and kept for future use after a small amount is used. With canned paste, spoon out unused portions in one-tablespoon amounts onto waxed paper and freeze, then lift the frozen paste off and store in a plastic container.

Vinegars

balsamic vinegar

Aged vinegar with a complex sweet and sour taste

red and white wine vinegars

tarragon vinegar

A white wine vinegar flavored with fresh tarragon, it is especially good in salads.

Wines and spirits

red wine, dry

sherry, dry

white wine, dry

IN THE REFRIGERATOR:

Basil

Though fresh basil is widely available only in summer, try to use it whenever possible to replace dried; the flavor is markedly superior. Stand the stems, preferably with roots intact, in a jar of water, and loosely cover leaves with a plastic bag.

Bread crumbs

You need never buy bread crumbs. To make fresh crumbs, use fresh or day-old bread and process in food processor or blender. For dried, toast bread 30 minutes in preheated 250-degree oven, turning occasionally to prevent slices from browning. Proceed as for fresh. Store bread crumbs in an airtight container: fresh crumbs in the refrigerator, and dried crumbs in a cool, dry place. Either type may also be frozen for several weeks if tightly wrapped in a plastic bag.

Butter

Many cooks prefer unsalted butter because of its finer flavor and because it does not burn as easily as salted.

Cheese

mozzarella

This versatile cheese is bland and semi-firm in its packaged form; freshly made mozzarella is moister and more delicate. Both melt superbly.

Parmesan

Avoid the pre-grated packaged variety; it is very expensive and almost flavorless. Buy Parmesan by the quarter- or half-pound wedge and grate as needed: 4 ounces produces about one cup of grated cheese.

Coriander

Also called *cilantro* or Chinese parsley, its pungent leaves resemble flat-leaf parsley. Keep in a glass of water covered with a plastic bag.

Cream

heavy cream

sour cream

Eggs

Will keep 4 to 5 weeks in refrigerator. For best results, bring to room temperature before using.

Lemons

In addition to its many uses in cooking, a slice of lemon rubbed over cut apples and pears will keep them from discoloring. Do not substitute bottled juice or lemon extract.

Milk

Mint

Fresh mint will keep for a week if wrapped in a damp paper towel and enclosed in a plastic bag.

Mustard

The recipes in this book call for Dijon mustard.

Parsley

The two most commonly available kinds of parsley are flat-leaved and curly; they can be used interchangeably when necessary. Flat-leaved parsley has a more distinctive flavor and is generally preferred in cooking. Curly parsley wilts less easily and is excellent for garnishing. Store parsley in a glass of water and cover loosely with a plastic bag. It will keep for a week in the refrigerator. Or wash and dry it, and refrigerate in a small plastic bag with a dry paper towel inside to absorb any moisture.

Scallions

Scallions have a mild onion flavor. Store wrapped in plastic.

Yogurt

A versatile milk product of custard-like consistency. For information on making yogurt at home, see the box on page 10.

Equipment

Proper cooking equipment makes the work light and is a good cook's most prized possession. You can cook expertly without a store-bought steamer or even a food processor, but basic pans, knives, and a few other items are indispensable. Below are the things you need—and some attractive options—for preparing the menus in this volume.

Pots and pans
Large kettle or stockpot with cover
3 skillets (large, medium, small) with covers, one nonaluminum
2 heavy-gauge sauté pans, 10 to 12 inches in diameter, with covers and ovenproof handles
3 saucepans with covers (1-, 2-, and 4-quart capacities)
  Choose heavy-gauge enameled cast-iron, plain cast-iron, aluminum-clad stainless steel, and aluminum (but you need at least one saucepan that is not aluminum). Best—but very expensive—is tin-lined copper.

Large, heavy-gauge roasting pan with rack
Broiler pan with rack
13 x 9 x 2-inch baking pan
Two 17 x 11-inch baking sheets
9-inch square baking dish
9-inch pie pan
Large flameproof casserole with tight-fitting cover
Flameproof glass or ceramic baking dish
Heatproof serving bowl
2 heatproof serving platters
Four 4-ounce ramekins or small custard cups
Salad bowl

Knives
  A carbon-steel knife takes a sharp edge but tends to rust. You must wash and dry it after each use; otherwise it can blacken foods and counter tops. Good-quality stainless-steel knives, frequently honed, are less trouble and will serve just as well in the home kitchen. Never put a fine knife in the dishwasher. Rinse it, dry it, and put it away—but not loose in a drawer. Knives will stay sharp and last a long time if they have their own storage rack.
Small paring knife
10-inch chef's knife
Bread knife (serrated blade)
Sharpening steel

Other cooking tools
2 sets of mixing bowls in graduated sizes, one set preferably glass or stainless steel
Colander with a round base (stainless steel, aluminum, or enamel)
2 strainers in fine and coarse mesh
2 sieves in fine and coarse mesh
2 sets of measuring cups and spoons in graduated sizes
  One for dry ingredients, another for shortenings and liquids.
Cooking spoon
Slotted spoon
Long-handled wooden spoons
Wooden spatula (for stirring hot ingredients)
2 metal spatulas, or turners (for lifting hot foods from pans)
Slotted spatula
Rubber or vinyl spatula (for folding in ingredients)
Rolling pin
Grater (metal, with several sizes of holes)
  A rotary grater is handy for hard cheese.
2 wire whisks
Pair of metal tongs
Metal skewers
Wooden board
Garlic press
Vegetable peeler
Mortar and pestle
Vegetable steamer
Ladle
Pastry brush for basting (a small, new paintbrush that is not nylon serves well)
Stiff-bristled brush
Vegetable brush
Cooling rack
Kitchen timer
Aluminum foil
Paper towels
Plastic wrap
Waxed paper
Brown paper bag

Kitchen string
Thin rubber gloves

Electric appliances
Food processor or blender
  A blender will do most of the work required in this volume, but a food processor will do it more quickly and in larger volume. A food processor should be considered a necessity, not a luxury, for anyone who enjoys cooking.
Electric mixer

Optional cooking tools
Salad spinner
Egg poacher
Small jar with tight-fitting lid
Melon baller
Salad servers
Citrus juicer
  Inexpensive glass kind from the dime store will do.
Nutmeg grater
Meat pounder
Zester
Roll of masking tape or white paper tape for labeling and dating

GRATER

COLANDER

STRAINER

FOOD PROCESSOR

RUBBER SPATULA

WHISK

MIXING BOWLS

VEGETABLE PEELER

METAL SPATULA

SHARPENING STEEL

CHEF'S KNIFE

PARING KNIFE

VEGETABLE STEAMER

TONGS

SLOTTED SPATULA

SAUCEPANS

SAUTÉ PAN

SKILLET

15

Susan DeRege

Susan DeRege teaches Italian cooking in New York City in the winter and travels to Italy in the summer to collect regional recipes. No visit is complete without stops along the Italian Riviera in such towns as Portofino, Santa Margherita, Recco, and Camogli. The three menus she offers here are inspired by the many meals she has enjoyed beside the Gulf of Genoa.

Menu 1 features a number of Genoese staples: fresh fish, eggplant, zucchini, bell peppers, and herbs such as rosemary, basil, and parsley. The herbed vegetable dish can be served with the fish main course or presented as a tempting appetizer. Susan DeRege likes to toss the potatoes in a fine virgin olive oil, preferably one produced in Liguria, the region that encompasses the Riviera.

A meal fit for company, Menu 2 features a rich and creamy pasta dish favored in Recco. Walnuts, pine nuts, heavy cream, butter, Parmesan cheese, garlic, and basil are the principal ingredients in the sauce. With the pasta the cook serves tuna steaks, which are marinated and then grilled.

Menu 3 offers an interesting lasagna, in which the flat noodles are layered with two sauces—pesto and béchamel. The accompanying light seafood salad of shrimp and squid (known in Italy as *insalata di frutti di mare*) is served chilled with a mustardy vinaigrette.

Casual pottery underscores the simplicity of this Mediterranean meal: wine-braised red snapper with plum tomatoes, herbed vegetables, and new red potatoes tossed with basil and olive oil.

17

Braised Red Snapper
Herbed Mixed Vegetables
New Potatoes with Basil

Braised whole red snapper, redolent of rosemary, is the focal point of this meal. If you cannot find snapper, sea bass, red mullet, ocean perch, or grouper would also be good.

For the best flavor contrast in the herbed vegetable recipe, be sure to follow the suggested order of layering the vegetables. You can assemble this dish early in the day, cover and refrigerate it, then bake it at dinner time.

WHAT TO DRINK

This menu demands a crisp white wine, preferably one with lots of fruit and acid. A Pinot Grigio or an Italian Sauvignon Blanc is an excellent choice.

SHOPPING LIST AND STAPLES

2- to 2½-pound whole fresh red snapper, cleaned and gutted
12 small new red potatoes (about 1¾ pounds total weight)
2 medium-size onions (about 1 pound total weight)
2 small Italian eggplants (about ½ pound total weight)
4 fresh plum tomatoes (about ¾ pound total weight), or
  16-ounce can plum tomatoes
Medium-size zucchini (about ½ pound)
Medium-size red bell pepper
Medium-size yellow bell pepper
2 small cloves garlic
Small bunch arugula (optional)
Small bunch fresh parsley
Small bunch fresh rosemary, or 1 teaspoon dried
Small bunch fresh basil, or 1 tablespoon dried
1 lemon (optional)
2 ounces Parmesan cheese
¾ cup good-quality olive oil, preferably virgin
2-ounce jar capers
¼ cup all-purpose flour
1 teaspoon dried oregano
4 bay leaves
Salt
Freshly ground black pepper
½ cup dry white wine

UTENSILS

Food processor or grater
Large heavy-gauge skillet
Small skillet
Shallow 15 x 10-inch glass or ceramic baking dish
11 x 7-inch baking dish
Medium-size saucepan with cover
Small strainer
Measuring cups and spoons
Chef's knife
Paring knife
Wooden spoon
2 wide metal spatulas
Vegetable brush
Vegetable peeler

START-TO-FINISH STEPS

1. Wash parsley, and fresh basil and rosemary if using, and dry with paper towels. Trim stems and discard. Chop enough parsley to measure 1 tablespoon for red snapper recipe and, if *not* using fresh basil, chop enough parsley to measure 2 tablespoons for potatoes recipe. If using fresh basil, set aside 2 sprigs for garnish, if desired, and chop enough leaves to measure ¼ cup for potatoes recipe. If using fresh rosemary, set aside 6 sprigs for red snapper recipe. Reserve remaining fresh herbs for another use. Crush dried oregano for vegetables recipe, and dried rosemary, if using, for red snapper recipe. Peel and mince enough garlic to measure 1 teaspoon each for red snapper and vegetables recipes.
2. Follow vegetables recipe steps 1 through 8.
3. Follow red snapper recipe steps 1 through 9.
4. While fish is baking, follow vegetables recipe steps 9 through 11.
5. While fish and vegetables are baking, follow potatoes recipe steps 1 through 3 and red snapper recipe steps 10 and 11.
6. Follow potatoes recipe step 4, red snapper recipe step 12, vegetables recipe step 12, and serve.

RECIPES

Braised Red Snapper

2- to 2½-pound whole fresh red snapper, cleaned and gutted
¼ cup good-quality olive oil, preferably virgin
¼ cup all-purpose flour
1 bay leaf

1 tablespoon capers
4 fresh plum tomatoes (about ¾ pound total weight), or
   16-ounce can plum tomatoes
½ cup dry white wine
1 teaspoon minced garlic
6 sprigs fresh rosemary, or 1 teaspoon dried, crushed
1 tablespoon chopped fresh parsley
Salt and freshly ground black pepper
3 sprigs arugula for garnish (optional)
1 lemon for garnish (optional)

1. Rinse cavity and outside of fish under cold running water, and pat fish dry with paper towels; set aside.
2. Heat oil over medium-high heat in heavy-gauge skillet large enough to accommodate the fish.
3. While oil is heating, place flour on large sheet of waxed paper and lightly dredge fish in flour.
4. When oil is hot but not smoking, carefully place fish in pan and cook about 1½ to 2 minutes on one side, or until lightly browned.
5. Using 2 wide metal spatulas, turn fish and cook another 1½ to 2 minutes.
6. Transfer fish to shallow 15 x 10-inch glass or ceramic baking dish and place bay leaf in cavity of fish.
7. Turn capers into small strainer and rinse under cold running water; set aside to drain.
8. If using fresh tomatoes, wash and dry with paper towels. If using canned, drain well, reserving juice for another use. Quarter tomatoes or, if large, cut into sixths and arrange around fish.
9. Pour wine over fish; sprinkle with capers, garlic, rosemary, parsley, ½ teaspoon salt, and pepper to taste. Cover baking dish with foil and bake in preheated 450-degree oven 25 to 35 minutes, or until fish is firm and flakes easily when tested with a toothpick.
10. If using arugula, wash, dry, and set aside.
11. If using lemon, wash and dry. Halve lengthwise and then cut one half into thin wedges; set aside. Reserve remaining half for another use.
12. Using 2 wide metal spatulas, transfer fish to serving platter. Arrange tomato wedges around fish and pour pan liquid around fish and over tomatoes. Serve garnished with arugula and lemon wedges, if desired.

Herbed Mixed Vegetables

2 small Italian eggplants (about ½ pound total weight)
Salt
1 each medium-size red and yellow bell pepper
Medium-size zucchini (about ½ pound)
2 medium-size onions (about 1 pound total weight)
2 ounces Parmesan cheese
¼ cup plus 1 tablespoon good-quality olive oil, preferably
   virgin
1 teaspoon minced garlic
1 teaspoon dried oregano, crushed
Freshly ground black pepper
1 tablespoon chopped fresh parsley
3 bay leaves

1. Preheat oven to 450 degrees.
2. Wash and dry eggplants. Remove stem ends from eggplants and discard. Cut enough eggplant crosswise into ¼-inch-thick rounds to measure 3 cups.
3. Arrange a single layer of eggplant slices on platter and sprinkle generously with salt. Cover with double thickness of paper towels and repeat with remaining eggplant. Top with another platter and place bag of flour or other weight on platter; set eggplant aside 10 minutes to allow salt to extract bitter juices.
4. Meanwhile, wash peppers and dry with paper towels. Slice off tops; core, seed, and remove membranes. Cut peppers crosswise into ¼-inch-thick rings; stack rings and cut into quarters. Measure 1 cup mixed peppers; set aside.
5. Scrub zucchini under cold running water and dry with paper towel. Trim ends and discard; do *not* peel. Cut enough zucchini crosswise into ¼-inch-thick slices to measure 1 cup; set aside.
6. Peel onions and cut enough crosswise into ¼-inch-thick slices to measure 2 cups; set aside.
7. Using food processor fitted with steel blade, or grater, grate enough Parmesan to measure 3 tablespoons.
8. Grease 11 x 7-inch baking dish with 1 tablespoon olive oil; set aside.
9. Rinse eggplant slices and pat dry with paper towels. Scatter eggplant over bottom of prepared baking dish. Top with onion slices, then cover with zucchini slices. Sprinkle with red and yellow peppers; set aside.
10. Heat remaining ¼ cup oil in small skillet over medium heat. Add garlic and sauté about 2 minutes, or until slightly golden.
11. Sprinkle vegetables with grated Parmesan, oregano, ¼ teaspoon salt, pepper to taste, parsley, and bay leaves. Drizzle with oil and garlic from skillet and bake, uncovered, 25 to 30 minutes, or until vegetables are tender.
12. Remove dish from oven, discard bay leaves, and serve.

New Potatoes with Basil

12 small new red potatoes (about 1¾ pounds total weight)
1 teaspoon salt
3 tablespoons good-quality olive oil, preferably virgin
¼ cup chopped fresh basil, or 1 tablespoon dried plus 2
   tablespoons chopped fresh parsley
2 sprigs fresh basil for garnish (optional)

1. Scrub potatoes under cold running water. Using vegetable peeler or paring knife, remove strip of peel from circumference of each potato to prevent splitting while cooking.
2. Combine potatoes, salt, and enough cold water to cover in medium-size saucepan, cover pan, and bring water to a boil over high heat.
3. When water boils, remove cover, reduce heat to medium-high, and cook potatoes 20 minutes, or until they can be easily pierced with tip of knife.
4. Drain water from pan. Add oil and chopped fresh basil, or dried basil and parsley, and toss. Transfer potatoes to serving dish and garnish with basil sprigs, if desired.

Grilled Tuna Steaks
Pasta with Walnut Sauce
Tomatoes with Basil Vinaigrette

For the pasta dish, use imported packaged *fusilli* or *tagliatelle*. Or, if you have the time, the cook recommends making fresh *trenette*. This eggless pasta, in the form of ½-inch-wide ribbons, is cut on one side with a knife and on the other with a crimped pasta cutter.

When preparing the tuna steaks, use a ridged cast-iron griddle or skillet, or a stove-top grill. If using a stove-top grill, do not pour the marinade over the fish while it is on the grill; rather, keep the marinade warm, then pour it over the fish at serving time.

Grilled tuna steaks with capers and pasta with walnut sauce are two classic Ligurian dishes. Serve the salad of sliced tomatoes and fresh basil vinaigrette with the meal or offer it as an appetizer.

WHAT TO DRINK

The cook suggests a fine Frascati to accompany this menu, but a top quality Orvieto or Soave would serve as well.

SHOPPING LIST AND STAPLES

Four ½- to ¾-inch-thick fresh tuna steaks (1 to 1¼ pounds total weight)
3 medium-size ripe tomatoes (about 1 pound total weight)
Small head escarole
2 small cloves garlic
Medium-size shallot
Small bunch fresh basil, or 2½ teaspoons dried plus small bunch fresh parsley

Small bunch fresh rosemary, or ½ teaspoon dried
2 lemons, plus 1 lemon (optional)
3 tablespoons milk
1 pint heavy cream
4 tablespoons salted butter
¼ pound Parmesan cheese, preferably imported
⅔ cup good-quality olive oil, approximately, preferably virgin
2 teaspoons corn oil
2 tablespoons red wine vinegar
2-ounce jar capers
¾ pound dried fusilli or tagliatelle, or fresh trenette
1 slice firm home-style white bread
4-ounce can walnut pieces
2-ounce jar pine nuts
Freshly grated nutmeg
Salt and freshly ground black pepper

UTENSILS

Food processor or blender
Nonaluminum stockpot
Large cast-iron skillet or griddle with ridges
13 x 9 x 2-inch glass or ceramic baking dish
Small heavy-gauge nonaluminum saucepan
Small bowl
Colander
Small strainer
Measuring cups and spoons
Chef's knife
Paring knife
2 wooden spoons
Metal spatula
Rubber spatula
Basting brush
Small jar with tight-fitting lid
Grater, if not using food processor

START-TO-FINISH STEPS

1. Wash and dry fresh basil or parsley, and fresh rosemary if using. Trim stem ends and discard. Chop enough rosemary to measure 1 teaspoon for tuna recipe. Chop enough basil to measure 2 tablespoons each for pasta and tomatoes recipes, or, if using dried basil, chop enough parsley to measure 1 tablespoon for pasta recipe. Reserve remaining herbs for another use. If *not* using fresh basil or rosemary, crush enough dried basil to measure ½ teaspoon for pasta recipe and 2 teaspoons for tomatoes recipe, and enough dried rosemary to measure ½ teaspoon for tuna recipe. Squeeze enough lemon juice to measure 2 tablespoons each for tuna and tomatoes recipes. Peel and mince

garlic for tuna and pasta recipes. Peel and mince shallot for tomatoes recipe.

2. Follow pasta recipe step 1 and tuna recipe steps 1 through 3.
3. Follow tomatoes recipe steps 1 through 3.
4. Follow pasta recipe steps 2 through 6.
5. Follow tuna recipe steps 4 through 7.
6. Follow pasta recipe steps 7 and 8.
7. While pasta is cooking, follow tuna recipe step 8.
8. Follow pasta recipe steps 9 and 10, tuna recipe step 9, tomatoes recipe step 4, and serve.

RECIPES

Grilled Tuna Steaks

1 tablespoon capers
Four ½- to ¾-inch-thick fresh tuna steaks (1 to 1¼ pounds total weight)
¼ cup good-quality olive oil, preferably virgin
2 tablespoons freshly squeezed lemon juice
1 teaspoon minced garlic
1 teaspoon chopped fresh rosemary, or ½ teaspoon dried, crushed
Salt and freshly ground black pepper
2 teaspoons corn oil
1 lemon for garnish (optional)

1. Rinse capers in small strainer under cold water; drain.
2. Rinse tuna steaks and dry with paper towels.
3. Combine capers, olive oil, lemon juice, garlic, rosemary, ½ teaspoon salt, and pepper to taste in 13 x 9 x 2-inch glass or ceramic baking dish. Arrange tuna steaks in a single layer in dish and set aside to marinate 30 minutes, turning steaks every 10 minutes.
4. Brush cast-iron skillet or griddle with oil and place over medium-high heat. Preheat oven to 200 degrees.
5. Place 4 dinner plates in oven to warm.
6. When oil begins to smoke, place tuna steaks on skillet or griddle, reserving marinade, and cook 4 minutes, or until fish pales at edges and bottoms of steaks are seared.
7. Meanwhile, wash and dry lemon, if using for garnish. Halve lengthwise, then cut one half into 4 wedges; set aside. Reserve remaining half for another use.
8. With metal spatula, carefully turn tuna steaks. Pour marinade over steaks and cook another 4 minutes.
9. Transfer tuna steaks to dinner plates and top each steak with pan drippings. Garnish each plate with a lemon wedge, if desired.

Pasta with Walnut Sauce

1 slice firm home-style white bread
3 tablespoons milk
1 cup walnut pieces
1 tablespoon pine nuts
1 tablespoon good-quality olive oil, preferably virgin
4 tablespoons salted butter
½ teaspoon minced garlic

Salt
1¼ cups heavy cream
Pinch of freshly grated nutmeg
Freshly ground black pepper
¼ pound Parmesan cheese, preferably imported
¾ pound dried fusilli or tagliatelle, or fresh trenette
2 tablespoons chopped fresh basil, or ½ teaspoon dried, crushed basil plus 1 tablespoon chopped fresh parsley

1. Trim crusts from bread and discard. Place bread in small bowl, add milk, and set aside for a few minutes.
2. Bring 5 quarts of water to a boil in nonaluminum stockpot over high heat.
3. Meanwhile, combine walnuts and pine nuts in food processor fitted with steel blade or in blender and process until finely chopped.
4. Squeeze milk out of bread and tear bread into bits. Add bread, oil, butter, garlic, and ½ teaspoon salt to chopped nuts, and process until pastelike.
5. Transfer mixture to small heavy-gauge nonaluminum saucepan. Stir in heavy cream, nutmeg, and pepper to taste, and cook over medium heat, stirring occasionally, 15 minutes. Rinse and dry food processor container.
6. Grate enough Parmesan to measure ¾ cup; set aside. Reserve remaining Parmesan for another use.
7. Add ½ cup Parmesan to saucepan and stir briefly; reduce heat to low and keep sauce warm.
8. Add 1 tablespoon salt and pasta to boiling water, and stir to separate pasta. Cook fusilli 7 minutes, tagliatelle 6 minutes, or fresh trenette 45 seconds, or until al dente.
9. Turn pasta into colander and drain.
10. Return pasta to stockpot, add fresh basil, or dried basil and parsley, and toss to combine. Add sauce and toss until pasta is evenly coated. Divide pasta among 4 dinner plates and serve with remaining cheese on the side.

Tomatoes with Basil Vinaigrette

Small head escarole
3 medium-size ripe tomatoes (about 1 pound total weight)
2 tablespoons red wine vinegar
2 tablespoons freshly squeezed lemon juice
1 teaspoon minced shallot
2 tablespoons chopped fresh basil, or 2 teaspoons dried, crushed
Salt and freshly ground black pepper
⅓ cup good-quality olive oil, preferably virgin

1. Wash and dry escarole. Stack several leaves, roll up lengthwise, and cut crosswise to measure 2 cups shreds. Divide shreds among 4 salad plates.
2. Wash and dry tomatoes. Core tomatoes and cut crosswise into ¼-inch-thick slices. Divide slices among escarole-lined plates, cover with plastic wrap, and refrigerate.
3. Combine vinegar, lemon juice, shallot, basil, ¼ teaspoon salt, and pepper to taste in small jar with tight-fitting lid, and shake well. Add oil and shake until well blended.
4. Just before serving, shake dressing to recombine and pour equal amount over each salad.

Seafood Salad
Lasagna with Pesto and Béchamel

Serve family or friends a delicious dinner of baked lasagna layered with béchamel and pesto and a chilled seafood salad tossed with lemon and mustard dressing. Garnish each plate with lemon wedges and parsley, if desired.

Seafood salad is a traditional favorite of fishermen along the Italian Riviera, who often prepare it fresh for lunch. For this salad, purchase precleaned fresh or frozen squid or, if you prefer, clean the squid yourself at home. To do this, hold the head of the squid with one hand, the body with the other, and firmly pull the head away from the body. Cut away the tentacles and discard the remainder of the head. Pull the transparent quill-like piece out of the body sac and discard it. Wash the squid thoroughly inside and out, and peel the skin away from the body and fins. If you buy fresh squid the day before you plan to use it, refrigerate it in cold salted water, but cook it within 24 hours of purchase.

Pesto (a blend of fresh basil, olive oil, pine nuts, and cheese) is a popular Ligurian sauce for pasta. Here the pesto alternates with a delicate cheese-enriched béchamel (white sauce) between layers of lasagna. If you like, use fresh lasagna, but remember that the fresh noodles will cook through in less than a minute. To save time, you can prepare the sauces a day ahead of serving, and assemble and bake the lasagna at mealtime.

WHAT TO DRINK

Greco di Tufo, a distinctive, full-flavored white wine from around Naples, is a good first choice here. Or try an Italian Pinot Bianco.

SHOPPING LIST AND STAPLES

1 pound medium-size squid, cleaned
¾ pound medium-size shrimp, peeled and deveined
Small head leaf lettuce
Small bunch celery
Small red bell pepper
3 large cloves garlic
Large bunch fresh basil
Small bunch fresh parsley
2 lemons, plus 1 lemon (optional)
3 cups milk
4 tablespoons unsalted butter
½ pound Parmesan cheese
2 ounces Sardo or Pecorino Romano cheese
1 cup good-quality olive oil, preferably virgin
1 tablespoon Dijon mustard
¾ pound dried lasagna
2-ounce jar pine nuts

23

3 tablespoons all-purpose flour
1 bay leaf
Freshly grated nutmeg
Salt
Freshly ground black and white pepper
5 whole black peppercorns

UTENSILS

Food processor or blender
Large stockpot with cover
Large saucepan
2 medium-size saucepans, 1 heavy-gauge nonaluminum
13 x 9 x 2-inch glass or ceramic baking dish
Large nonaluminum bowl
Medium-size bowl
Small nonaluminum bowl
Colander
Measuring cups and spoons
Chef's knife
Paring knife
2 wooden spoons
Whisk
Metal spatula
Rubber spatula
Grater (if not using food processor)

START-TO-FINISH STEPS

1. Grate enough Parmesan cheese to measure 1¼ cups and enough Sardo or Pecorino Romano to measure 3 tablespoons for lasagna recipe; set aside separately. Prepare fresh herbs for all recipes.
2. Follow seafood salad recipe steps 1 through 6.
3. Follow lasagna recipe steps 1 through 7.
4. While lasagna is cooking, follow seafood salad recipe steps 7 through 10.
5. Follow lasagna recipe steps 8 through 13.
6. While lasagna is baking, follow seafood salad recipe steps 11 through 17.
7. Follow lasagna recipe step 14, seafood salad recipe step 18, and serve.

RECIPES

Seafood Salad

1 pound medium-size squid, cleaned and with tentacles separated
Salt
1 bay leaf
5 whole black peppercorns
¾ pound medium-size shrimp, peeled and deveined
2 stalks celery
Small red bell pepper
2 lemons, plus 1 lemon for garnish (optional)
1 tablespoon Dijon mustard
Freshly ground black pepper
½ cup good-quality olive oil, preferably virgin

3 tablespoons chopped fresh parsley, plus 4 sprigs for garnish (optional)
Small head leaf lettuce

1. Rinse squid thoroughly under cold running water, then cut crosswise into ½-inch-thick slices. Chop tentacles coarsely. Place in medium-size bowl with 1 tablespoon salt and enough cold water to cover; set aside.
2. Combine 1 quart water, bay leaf, and peppercorns in medium-size saucepan and bring to a boil over high heat.
3. Meanwhile, bring 2 quarts water to a boil in large saucepan over high heat.
4. Add 1 teaspoon salt and shrimp to boiling water in medium-size saucepan, return to a boil, and cook 2 minutes, or just until shrimp turn pink.
5. Meanwhile, add 1 teaspoon salt and squid to boiling water in large saucepan, reduce heat to medium, and simmer 15 minutes, or just until tender. Do *not* overcook or squid will become tough.
6. Turn shrimp into colander and place under cold running water to cool.
7. Transfer shrimp to double thickness of paper towels and pat dry.
8. Turn squid into colander and set under cold running water to cool.
9. Wash and dry celery. Cut enough celery crosswise into ¼-inch-thick slices to measure 1 cup; set aside.
10. Wash and dry bell pepper. Halve, core, and seed pepper. Cut lengthwise into ¼-inch-wide strips; set aside.
11. Squeeze enough lemon juice to measure ⅓ cup.
12. Combine lemon juice, mustard, ½ teaspoon salt, and pepper to taste in small nonaluminum bowl, and whisk until blended.
13. Whisking continuously, slowly add olive oil and whisk until dressing is blended and smooth; set aside.
14. Transfer squid to double thickness of paper towels and pat dry.
15. Combine squid, shrimp, celery, bell pepper, and chopped parsley in large nonaluminum bowl. Add dressing and toss to combine. Cover with plastic wrap and refrigerate until ready to serve.
16. Meanwhile, wash and dry lettuce. Remove and discard any bruised or discolored leaves. Using 1 or 2 large leaves for each, form beds for salad on 4 dinner plates. Reserve remaining lettuce for another use.
17. If using lemon for garnish, wash and dry with paper towel. Halve lengthwise, then cut each half into 4 wedges.
18. Just before serving, top lettuce with equal portions of chilled salad and garnish each serving with lemon wedges and a sprig of parsley, if desired.

Lasagna with Pesto and Béchamel

1 tablespoon salt
¾ pound dried lasagna

Pesto:
3 large cloves garlic
3 cups firmly packed fresh basil leaves

3 tablespoons pine nuts
½ cup virgin olive oil, approximately
1 tablespoon unsalted butter
½ teaspoon each salt and freshly ground black pepper
¾ cup freshly grated Parmesan cheese
3 tablespoons freshly grated Sardo or Pecorino Romano cheese

Béchamel:
3 tablespoons unsalted butter
3 tablespoons all-purpose flour
3 cups milk
Pinch of salt
Pinch of freshly grated nutmeg
½ teaspoon freshly ground white pepper
½ cup freshly grated Parmesan cheese

1. Bring 4½ quarts water to a boil in large covered stockpot over high heat.
2. Meanwhile, prepare pesto: Crush garlic under flat blade of chef's knife; remove peels and discard.
3. In food processor fitted with steel blade or in blender, chop basil leaves, turning machine on and off a few times.
4. With machine running, add garlic and process until finely chopped. Add pine nuts and continue to process. Add oil, butter, salt, and pepper, and process until mixture is smooth and pastelike.
5. Stir in cheeses. If using processor, quickly blend in cheeses to maintain pastelike consistency; set pesto aside.
6. Add 1 tablespoon salt to boiling water in stockpot, add lasagna, and cook about 7 minutes, or until *al dente.*
7. Fill 13 x 9 x 2-inch glass or ceramic baking dish half full with cold water; set aside.
8. Drain lasagna in colander and carefully transfer to baking dish of cold water to prevent sticking. Arrange cooled lasagna in single layer on damp kitchen towel or jelly-roll pan and set aside. Dry baking dish; set aside.
9. Preheat oven to 450 degrees.
10. For béchamel, melt butter in medium-size heavy-gauge nonaluminum saucepan over medium heat. Whisk in flour and bring to a gentle simmer, whisking continuously. Simmer 2 minutes; do *not* allow to brown.
11. Add milk and seasonings, and whisk until blended. Increase heat to medium-high and, whisking continuously, bring mixture to a boil. Reduce heat and simmer, whisking occasionally, 5 minutes. Remove pan from heat.
12. Add ¼ cup Parmesan to béchamel and whisk until blended. Cover surface of sauce with plastic wrap to prevent skin from forming; set aside.
13. Butter baking dish. Cover bottom of prepared dish with a single layer of lasagna (about 6 strips). Spread half of the béchamel over lasagna, then top with another layer of lasagna. Spread pesto evenly over lasagna, then cover with another layer of lasagna. Top with remaining béchamel, sprinkle evenly with remaining ¼ cup Parmesan, and bake in center of oven 15 to 20 minutes, or until béchamel is golden and lasagna is heated through.
14. Cut lasagna into squares and, using metal spatula, transfer to dinner plates.

ADDED TOUCH
The rich fruity flavor of amaretto, an Italian almond liqueur, enhances this delightful dessert.

Peach Cake with Toasted Almonds

4 ripe freestone peaches (about 1½ pounds total weight), or 1-pound can sliced peaches
¼ cup sliced blanched almonds
Large lemon

Batter:
⅓ cup unsalted butter, at room temperature
⅔ cup granulated sugar
⅔ cup milk
1 tablespoon amaretto or other almond-flavored liqueur
1 teaspoon vanilla extract
2 eggs, at room temperature
1 teaspoon baking powder
1½ cups all-purpose flour
Pinch of salt

1 tablespoon granulated sugar
1 tablespoon unsalted butter, cut into bits

1. Preheat oven to 375 degrees.
2. If using fresh peaches, bring 1 quart water to a boil in medium-size saucepan over high heat.
3. Meanwhile, butter 1-quart round baking dish or 9-inch pie pan; set aside.
4. Spread almonds in baking dish and toast in oven, shaking dish occasionally to prevent scorching, 8 to 10 minutes, or until almonds are light golden.
5. Plunge peaches into boiling water and blanch 1 minute to loosen skins. Turn into colander and cool under cold running water.
6. Wash lemon and dry with paper towel. Grate enough rind, avoiding white pith as much as possible, to measure 2 teaspoons; set aside. Halve lemon and squeeze juice; set aside.
7. Remove almonds from oven and set aside to cool.
8. Remove skins from peaches and discard. Halve each peach lengthwise and twist halves to separate. Remove pits and discard. Cut peaches lengthwise into ½-inch-thick slices and place in medium-size nonaluminum bowl. Sprinkle with lemon juice to prevent discoloration and toss gently until evenly coated; set aside. If using canned sliced peaches, turn into strainer set over medium-size bowl and set aside to drain.
9. Combine butter and sugar in medium-size mixing bowl and cream together until light and fluffy.
10. Add remaining batter ingredients and stir until well blended.
11. Turn batter into prepared baking pan and smooth top. Top batter with peaches, arranging them in a decorative pattern, and then top with almonds. Sprinkle cake evenly with sugar and butter, and bake 30 to 35 minutes, or until firm to the touch. Serve directly from pan.

Maria and Guy Reuge

M aria and Guy Reuge work well in tandem despite their very different culinary backgrounds (she learned to cook in the American South, he in France). When they collaborate on menu planning, the resultant meals are often eclectic—and always delicious. Having traveled together frequently in the south of France, they are united in their particular fondness for the foods of that area. Here they offer some dishes that are classically French and others that are Guy Reuge's own interpretations.

The Reuges describe Menu 1 as Provençal, except for the recipe for stuffed eggs with salmon caviar and anchovies, which comes from the principality of Monaco. The entrée is a generous portion of monkfish sauced with a mixture of tomatoes and shallots (a classic Provençal touch) and served with braised fennel.

Menu 2 features two dishes popular in Languedoc: mussels stuffed with an herb-and-almond butter and pork chops with anchovy sauce. The accompanying zucchini sticks are sautéed quickly to preserve their bright green color.

The cooks' third menu, also from Provence, is extremely adaptable to what is best in the market. For example, in the herbed goat cheese salad you can use another soft-leafed lettuce in place of the *mâche* (lamb's lettuce), which is often hard to find. For the seafood stew, select the best and freshest firm-fleshed white fish available.

A Monégasque specialty—stuffed eggs garnished with caviar and anchovies—is paired with sautéed monkfish in a chunky tomato sauce and braised fennel bulbs, two dishes popular in Provence. Serve the eggs as a first course, if desired.

Eggs Monégasque
Monkfish Provençal
Braised Fennel

Because it has firm, sweet flesh resembling that of lobster, inexpensive monkfish is increasingly popular in this country. Also marketed as goosefish or anglerfish, monkfish is available on the Atlantic and Gulf coasts but is not often sold elsewhere. Suitable alternatives are scrod and halibut. Dusting the fish fillets with flour gives them a golden color when sautéed.

Fresh fennel, also known as *finocchio*, has feathery green leaves topping a bulbous base; its anise flavor, which mellows when the bulbs are braised, is a good complement for fish. Select bulbs that are pale green, firm, and have no soft or brownish spots. Fennel is sold in Italian groceries and well-stocked supermarkets during the fall and winter. If necessary, you can substitute the same amount of sliced celery plus one-half teaspoon fennel seeds, but the flavor will not be quite the same.

WHAT TO DRINK

The cooks suggest a white wine from the Côtes de Provence as an ideal accompaniment for this menu. Or, try a white Châteauneuf-du-Pape.

SHOPPING LIST AND STAPLES

4 monkfish fillets (about 2 pounds total weight)
4 small or 2 large fennel bulbs (about 2 pounds total weight)
1 large plus 4 medium-size ripe tomatoes (about 2¾ pounds total weight), or 1 large ripe tomato plus 14-ounce can plum tomatoes
Small head red leaf lettuce
3 medium-size shallots
Small clove garlic
1 bunch parsley
1½ cups chicken stock, preferably homemade (see page 9), or canned
5 large eggs
1 stick plus 1 tablespoon unsalted butter
2 tablespoons good-quality olive oil
¼ cup mayonnaise
2-ounce tin flat anchovy fillets
4-ounce jar salmon caviar
¼ cup all-purpose flour, approximately
Salt
Freshly ground pepper

UTENSILS

Large heavy-gauge nonaluminum skillet with cover
Medium-size nonaluminum skillet with cover
Large saucepan
Medium-size saucepan
1½-quart flameproof casserole with cover
9-inch pie pan (optional)
Heatproof platter
Medium-size bowl
Small bowl
Colander
Sieve
Measuring cups and spoons
Chef's knife
Paring knife
Wooden spoon
Slotted spoon
Slotted spatula
Whisk
Pastry bag fitted with medium-size fluted tip (optional)

START-TO-FINISH STEPS

One hour ahead: Set out eggs to come to room temperature.

1. Follow monkfish recipe step 1 and fennel recipe steps 1 through 4.
2. While fennel is baking, follow eggs recipe steps 1 and 2 and monkfish recipe steps 2 through 5.
3. Follow eggs recipe step 3 and monkfish recipe step 6.
4. Follow eggs recipe steps 4 through 10.
5. Follow monkfish recipe steps 7 through 9.
6. Follow fennel recipe steps 5 through 8.
7. While liquid is reducing, follow monkfish recipe steps 10 through 13.
8. Follow fennel recipe step 9 and monkfish recipe steps 14 and 15.
9. Follow fennel recipe step 10, monkfish recipe step 16, and serve with eggs.

RECIPES

Eggs Monégasque

5 large eggs
¼ cup mayonnaise

Small head red leaf lettuce
Large ripe tomato
4 anchovy fillets
4-ounce jar salmon caviar

1. Place eggs in medium-size saucepan, add enough cold water to cover, and bring to a boil over high heat. Boil eggs, stirring occasionally, 10 minutes. Stirring will keep the yolks centered.
2. Half-fill medium-size bowl with cold water; set aside.
3. Drain eggs and transfer to bowl of cold water.
4. When cool, peel eggs, halve lengthwise, and remove yolks. Force 4 yolks and 1 whole hard-boiled egg through sieve into small bowl. Reserve remaining egg white halves.
5. Add mayonnaise to sieved eggs and stir to combine.
6. If desired, transfer egg mixture to pastry bag fitted with medium-size fluted tip and pipe decoratively into reserved egg white halves. Or, spoon mixture into egg white halves. Place stuffed eggs on plate, cover with plastic wrap, and refrigerate.
7. Meanwhile, wash lettuce and dry with paper towels. Remove and discard any bruised or discolored leaves. Using 1 or 2 leaves for each, line 4 individual salad plates with lettuce; set aside. Reserve remaining lettuce for another use.
8. Wash and dry tomato. Core tomato and cut crosswise into 8 slices. Divide among lettuce-lined plates.
9. Drain anchovies and split lengthwise; set aside.
10. Divide stuffed eggs among prepared plates and top each egg half with 1 anchovy strip and some salmon caviar. Cover and refrigerate until ready to serve.

Monkfish Provençal

4 medium-size ripe tomatoes (about 2 pounds total weight), or 14-ounce can plum tomatoes
3 medium-size shallots
Small clove garlic
1 bunch parsley
¼ cup all-purpose flour, approximately
4 monkfish fillets (about 2 pounds total weight)
2 tablespoons good-quality olive oil
4 tablespoons unsalted butter
Salt and freshly ground pepper

1. If using fresh tomatoes, bring 2 quarts water to a boil in large saucepan over high heat.
2. Peel and mince enough shallots to measure 3 tablespoons.
3. Peel and mince enough garlic to measure 1 teaspoon.
4. Plunge tomatoes into boiling water and blanch 15 seconds.
5. Transfer tomatoes to colander and cool under cold running water.
6. Wash parsley and dry with paper towels. Trim stems and discard. Mince enough parsley to measure ¾ cup; set aside. Reserve remainder for another use.
7. Peel, core, halve, and seed tomatoes. Coarsely chop

enough to measure 4 cups; set aside.
8. Place flour in pie pan or on sheet of waxed paper.
9. Rinse fish under cold running water and dry with paper towels. Cut each fillet on diagonal into 1-inch-wide slices.
10. Heat oil in large heavy-gauge nonaluminum skillet over high heat until very hot but not smoking.
11. Working quickly, lightly dredge each piece of fish in flour, gently shake off excess, and add to skillet. Fry 1½ minutes per side, or until golden brown.
12. With slotted spatula, transfer monkfish to heatproof platter, cover loosely with foil, and keep warm in 200-degree oven.
13. Place 4 dinner plates in oven to warm.
14. Pour off oil from skillet, add butter, and heat over medium-high heat until butter starts to sizzle.
15. Add shallots, garlic, parsley, tomatoes, and any juices that have accumulated on platter with fish, and stir to combine. Stir in salt and pepper to taste. Cover skillet, remove from heat, and keep warm until ready to serve.
16. Divide sauce among dinner plates, top with fish, and serve.

Braised Fennel

4 small or 2 large fennel bulbs (about 2 pounds total weight)
1½ cups chicken stock
5 tablespoons unsalted butter
Salt and freshly ground pepper

1. Preheat oven to 400 degrees.
2. Rinse and dry fennel. Remove stalks and trim bottom of bulbs. Set aside 8 feathery tops for garnish and discard remaining trimmings. If using small bulbs, halve lengthwise; if using large bulbs, cut into quarters. Set aside.
3. Cut out waxed-paper disk large enough to cover 1½-quart flameproof casserole and butter 1 side; set aside.
4. Combine fennel, stock, 1 tablespoon butter, and salt and pepper to taste in flameproof casserole and bring to a boil over high heat. Top casserole with prepared waxed paper, cover, and bake 40 minutes.
5. Remove fennel from oven and reduce oven temperature to 200 degrees, leaving oven door ajar for a few minutes to reduce temperature more rapidly.
6. Meanwhile, drain cooking liquid into medium-size non-aluminum skillet. Return covered casserole with fennel to 200-degree oven and keep warm until ready to serve.
7. Cut remaining butter into bits; set aside.
8. Bring liquid in skillet to a boil over high heat. Lower heat to medium and simmer 4 to 5 minutes, or until liquid is reduced to about 1 tablespoon.
9. Add butter, a few bits at a time, to reduced cooking liquid, whisking after each addition, until butter is totally incorporated and sauce is thick and smooth. Add salt and pepper to taste. Cover pan, remove from heat, and keep sauce warm until ready to serve.
10. Divide fennel among 4 dinner plates, top with equal portions of sauce, and garnish each serving with feathery fennel tops.

Mussels Stuffed with Herbed Almond Butter
Pork Chops with Anchovy Sauce
Sautéed Zucchini Sticks

Herbed mussels arranged pinwheel-style go well with pork chops with anchovy sauce and sautéed zucchini sticks.

The thick meaty pork chops are served with a pungent anchovy sauce. Be sure to chill the butter thoroughly before adding it to the deglazed pan juices. Adding the butter bit by bit and then whisking rapidly ensures that the sauce emulsifies properly and achieves a smooth, velvety texture.

Since zucchini is often watery, you might want to salt the sticks before sautéing them, then allow them to rest for half an hour to extract excess moisture. Before cooking, blot the squash with paper towels. If you are on a salt-free diet, rinse off the salt before patting the sticks dry.

WHAT TO DRINK

A light red wine, such as a simple Côtes du Rhône or a Beaujolais, is in order here. White wine enthusiasts may prefer a well-chilled Gewürztraminer with these dishes.

SHOPPING LIST AND STAPLES

Four ¾-inch-thick loin pork chops (about 2 pounds total weight)
1¾ pounds mussels (about 2 dozen)
2 medium-size zucchini (about 1 pound total weight)
3 shallots
Small clove garlic
Small bunch fresh parsley
Small bunch fresh thyme, or ½ teaspoon dried
1 lemon, plus 2 lemons (optional)
1 orange (optional)
½ cup beef stock, preferably homemade, or canned
1 stick plus 1 tablespoon unsalted butter
1 tablespoon good-quality olive oil
2-ounce tin flat anchovy fillets
¼ cup all-purpose flour
3½-ounce can sliced blanched almonds
Salt and freshly ground pepper
1 cup dry white wine, approximately

UTENSILS

Food processor or blender
Large nonaluminum kettle or stockpot with cover
Large heavy-gauge nonaluminum skillet
Medium-size skillet or sauté pan with cover
13 x 9 x 2-inch baking dish
9-inch pie pan (optional)
Large bowl
Small bowl
Large sieve
Measuring cups and spoons
Chef's knife
Paring knife
Wooden spoon
Rubber spatula
Metal spatula
Whisk
Metal tongs

Vegetable brush
Stiff-bristled brush
Vegetable peeler

START-TO-FINISH STEPS

One hour ahead: Set out butter to come to room temperature for pork chops recipe.

1. Wash parsley and dry with paper towels. Trim stems and discard. Set aside ⅓ cup loosely packed sprigs for mussels recipe, and 4 sprigs if using for garnish for pork chops recipe. Mince enough parsley to measure 1 tablespoon for pork chops recipe. If using fresh thyme for zucchini recipe, rinse and pat dry. Mince enough thyme leaves to measure 1 teaspoon.
2. Follow mussels recipe steps 1 through 11.
3. Follow pork chops recipe steps 1 through 5.
4. While pork chops are browning, follow mussels recipe step 12.
5. Follow pork chops recipe steps 6 through 11 and zucchini recipe step 1.
6. Follow mussels recipe step 13.
7. While mussels are baking, follow pork chops recipe steps 12 and 13 and zucchini recipe steps 2 and 3.
8. Follow mussels recipe step 14, pork chops recipe step 14, and serve with zucchini.

RECIPES

Mussels Stuffed with Herbed Almond Butter

1¾ pounds mussels (about 2 dozen)
3 shallots
½ cup dry white wine
Small clove garlic
1 lemon, plus 2 lemons for garnish (optional)
⅓ cup loosely packed parsley sprigs
4 tablespoons unsalted butter
2 tablespoons sliced blanched almonds
¼ teaspoon freshly ground pepper

1. Preheat oven to 400 degrees.
2. Using stiff-bristled brush, scrub mussels under cold running water, remove beards, and rinse. Remove and discard any cracked or open mussels; set remainder aside.
3. Peel and mince enough shallots to measure ⅓ cup.
4. Combine mussels, shallots, and white wine in large nonaluminum kettle or stockpot and steam, covered, over high heat 4 minutes, shaking pan 2 or 3 times.
5. Meanwhile, crush garlic under flat blade of chef's knife. Remove peel and discard.
6. Squeeze enough lemon juice to measure 1 tablespoon.
7. Turn mussels into large sieve set over large bowl to drain. Return mussel liquor to kettle or stockpot and bring to a boil over high heat. Boil 2 to 3 minutes, or until liquid is reduced to about 1 tablespoon.
8. Meanwhile, mince garlic and parsley in food processor fitted with steel blade or in blender.

9. With machine running, add butter, 1 tablespoon at a time, and process until totally incorporated.

10. Add the reduced mussel liquor, lemon juice, almonds, and pepper, and process until herbed almond butter is well blended and smooth; set aside.

11. Remove and discard any unopened mussels. Remove and discard top shells from remaining mussels, leaving meat in bottom shells. Top each mussel with about 2 teaspoons of herbed almond butter, mounding it slightly, and arrange stuffed mussels in a single layer in 13 x 9 x 2-inch baking dish; set aside.

12. If using lemons for garnish, wash under cold running water and dry. Cut crosswise into thin slices. Divide slices among 4 salad plates; set aside.

13. When ready to serve, bake mussels 5 to 7 minutes, or until butter is just melted.

14. Divide mussels among prepared plates and serve.

Pork Chops with Anchovy Sauce

4 to 6 anchovy fillets
4 tablespoons unsalted butter, at room temperature
¼ cup all-purpose flour
1 tablespoon good-quality olive oil
Four ¾-inch-thick loin pork chops (about 2 pounds total weight)
1 orange for garnish (optional)
⅓ cup dry white wine
½ cup beef stock
Freshly ground pepper
1 tablespoon minced fresh parsley, plus 4 sprigs parsley for garnish (optional)

1. Drain anchovies, rinse under cold running water, and pat dry with paper towels.

2. Combine anchovies and butter in food processor fitted with steel blade or in blender and process until smooth. Turn mixture into small bowl, cover with plastic wrap, and refrigerate.

3. Place flour in pie pan or on sheet of waxed paper.

4. Heat oil in large heavy-gauge nonaluminum skillet over medium-high heat until hot but not smoking.

5. Dry pork chops with paper towels. Working quickly, dredge chops with flour, gently shake off excess, and add chops to skillet. Brown 4 minutes on one side.

6. Using tongs, turn chops and brown another 4 minutes.

7. Meanwhile, cut chilled anchovy butter into bits.

8. Wash and dry orange if using for garnish. Using sharp paring knife or vegetable peeler, cut four ½-inch-wide strips of peel. Reserve orange for another use.

9. Transfer chops to platter, cover loosely with foil, and keep warm on stove top.

10. Pour off fat from skillet. Add wine and bring to a boil over medium-high heat, stirring and scraping up any browned bits clinging to bottom of pan.

11. Add stock and boil mixture 3 to 4 minutes, or until reduced to about 2 tablespoons.

12. Reduce heat under skillet to low. Add anchovy butter to skillet, a few bits at a time, whisking until butter is

totally incorporated; simmer gently 1 to 2 minutes, or until sauce is thickened.

13. Add pepper to taste, remove sauce from heat, and keep warm on stove top.

14. Divide pork chops among 4 dinner plates. Top with sauce, sprinkle with minced parsley, and serve with a twist of orange rind and a sprig of parsley, if desired.

Sautéed Zucchini Sticks

2 medium-size zucchini (about 1 pound total weight)
1 tablespoon unsalted butter
1 teaspoon minced fresh thyme, or ½ teaspoon dried, crushed
Salt and freshly ground pepper

1. Using vegetable brush, scrub zucchini under cold running water, rinse, and dry with paper towels. Trim but do not peel. Cut each zucchini crosswise into 4 pieces, then halve each piece lengthwise. Cut each piece lengthwise again into ¼-inch-wide sticks; set aside.

2. Heat butter in medium-size skillet or sauté pan over medium-high heat just until it starts to sizzle. Add zucchini and sauté, stirring and tossing, 3 minutes.

3. Add thyme, and salt and pepper to taste, and toss to combine. Cover pan, remove from heat, and set aside until ready to serve.

ADDED TOUCH

For these thin apple tarts, use puff pastry, either freshly made or purchased frozen from the supermarket.

Honey-Glazed Apple Tarts

1-pound package frozen puff pastry, thawed
4 baking apples, preferably Granny Smith
4 teaspoons unsalted butter
2 tablespoons granulated sugar
¼ cup honey

1. Divide puff pastry into quarters. On lightly floured surface, roll each quarter into ⅛-inch-thick round.

2. Place a 6- to 8-inch round plate, face down, over each round and cut around plate with paring knife. Carefully transfer 4 dough circles to 2 baking sheets, cover with plastic wrap, and chill 1 hour.

3. Peel, core, and halve apples. Cut lengthwise into ⅛-inch-thick slices. You should have about 5 cups.

4. Preheat oven to 400 degrees.

5. Remove dough circles from refrigerator and prick with fork. Arrange apple slices in concentric circles on dough; dot each tart with 1 teaspoon butter and sprinkle with ½ tablespoon sugar. Bake 15 to 20 minutes, or until crust is golden.

6. While tarts are baking, heat honey in small saucepan over medium heat about 1 minute, or until warm and slightly runny.

7. Remove tarts from oven and brush with honey. Serve warm.

Herbed Goat Cheese Salad
Provençal Fish Stew

A one-pot seafood stew, fragrant with garlic, wine, and saffron, is accompanied by a mildly tart goat cheese salad.

For the fish stew, select any available variety of firm-fleshed fish: Swordfish could be substituted for the shark, and scrod for the monkfish. Shark—still a bargain—is a firm, dry, delicately flavored fish that many Americans have yet to discover. The most popular variety is the dark-fleshed mako.

Saffron, which colors and flavors the stew, is a pungent and expensive spice frequently used in Mediterranean cooking. Fortunately, a little goes a long way; a quarter of a teaspoon is ample for this recipe. Shop for saffron in specialty food stores or good supermarkets, but avoid a product call Mexican saffron—it is, in fact, safflower.

WHAT TO DRINK

A southern French rosé is a natural choice with a Provençal chowder. The very best is Tavel, but almost any rosé from Provence or the Rhône Valley would be good.

SHOPPING LIST AND STAPLES

12 littleneck clams (about 1 pound total weight)
12 mussels (about ¾ pound total weight)
8 medium-size shrimp (about ½ pound total weight)

¼-pound monkfish fillet
¼-pound sea bass fillet
¼-pound mako shark steak
1 head Boston lettuce
Small head red leaf lettuce
Small bunch mâche (optional)
Small head radicchio (optional)
2 medium-size ripe tomatoes, or 8¼-ounce can
   plum tomatoes
2 medium-size onions (about 1 pound total weight)
2 small cloves garlic
Small bunch parsley
1 egg
1 pint heavy cream
8-ounce log Montrachet or other soft goat cheese
5 tablespoons good-quality olive oil
1 tablespoon red wine vinegar
¼ teaspoon Dijon mustard
Hot pepper sauce
Small loaf French or Italian bread
¼ teaspoon saffron threads
Salt
Freshly ground pepper
Coarsely ground black pepper
½ cup dry white wine

UTENSILS

Large nonaluminum sauté pan or large deep non-
   aluminum skillet with cover
Small flameproof skillet or small baking sheet
Medium-size saucepan
Broiler pan with rack
Large bowl
Small nonaluminum bowl
Salad spinner (optional)
Colander
Measuring cups and spoons
Chef's knife
Serrated bread knife (optional)
Paring knife
Wooden spoon
Slotted spoon
Wide metal spatula
Whisk
Pastry brush
Stiff-bristled brush

START-TO-FINISH STEPS

1. Follow salad recipe steps 1 through 7.
2. Follow stew recipe steps 1 through 13 and salad recipe steps 8 and 9.
3. Follow stew recipe steps 14 and 15.
4. While broth reduces, follow salad recipe steps 10 through 12.
5. Follow stew recipe step 16 and salad recipe step 13.
6. Follow stew recipe step 17 and serve with salad.

RECIPES

Herbed Goat Cheese Salad

1 head Boston lettuce
Small head red leaf lettuce
Small bunch mâche (optional)
Small head radicchio (optional)
1 egg
¼ teaspoon Dijon mustard
1 tablespoon red wine vinegar
Salt
Freshly ground pepper
¼ cup good-quality olive oil
1 tablespoon heavy cream
Small clove garlic
Small loaf French or Italian bread
8-ounce log Montrachet or other soft goat cheese
½ teaspoon coarsely ground black pepper

1. Wash Boston and red leaf lettuces, and mâche and radicchio if using, in several changes of water and dry in salad spinner or with paper towels. Remove and discard any bruised or discolored leaves. Reserve half of red leaf lettuce for another use. Tear remaining salad greens and radicchio into bite-size pieces and combine in large bowl. Cover bowl with plastic wrap and refrigerate until ready to serve.

Boston lettuce

Mâche   *Radicchio*

2. Separate egg, placing yolk in small nonaluminum bowl and reserving white for another use.
3. Add mustard, vinegar, and salt and pepper to taste to yolk, and whisk until blended.
4. Whisking continuously, gradually add 3 tablespoons oil and whisk until dressing is thick and smooth. Add cream and whisk until blended. Cover bowl with plastic wrap and refrigerate until ready to serve.
5. Crush garlic under flat blade of chef's knife; remove peel and discard. Set garlic aside.
6. Cut four ½-inch-thick slices from bread; reserve remaining bread for another use.

7. Rub cut sides of bread with crushed garlic and brush with half of remaining olive oil; set aside.

8. Preheat broiler.

9. Cut cheese crosswise into four 1½-inch-thick slices. Brush cheese slices with remaining olive oil and sprinkle with coarsely ground pepper.

10. Arrange cheese slices in a single layer in small flameproof skillet or on baking sheet and broil about 2½ inches from heating element 2 to 3 minutes, or just until bubbly.

11. While cheese is broiling, place bread around it on broiler rack to toast.

12. Meanwhile, whisk dressing to recombine and pour over salad. Toss salad until evenly coated and divide among 4 salad plates.

13. Transfer toasts to salad plates. Using metal spatula, top each toast with a slice of cheese.

Provençal Fish Stew

2 medium-size ripe tomatoes, or 8¼-ounce can plum tomatoes
Small clove garlic
2 medium-size onions (about 1 pound total weight)
8 medium-size shrimp (about ½ pound total weight)
12 littleneck clams (about 1 pound total weight)
12 mussels (about ¾ pound total weight)
¼-pound monkfish fillet
¼-pound sea bass fillet
¼-pound mako shark steak
1 tablespoon good-quality olive oil
Small bunch parsley
¼ teaspoon saffron threads
½ cup dry white wine
Hot pepper sauce
1 cup heavy cream
Salt
Freshly ground pepper

1. If using fresh tomatoes, bring 1 quart of water to a boil in medium-size saucepan over high heat.

2. Meanwhile, peel garlic and mince enough to measure 1 teaspoon; set aside.

3. Plunge fresh tomatoes into boiling water and blanch 15 seconds. Transfer tomatoes to colander and cool under cold running water. Peel, core, halve, and seed tomatoes.

Squeeze out seeds with one hand.

Coarsely chop enough fresh tomatoes to measure 1 cup. If using canned tomatoes, drain and chop enough to measure 1 cup; set aside.

4. Halve, peel, and chop enough onion to measure 2 cups; set aside.

5. Pinch off legs of shrimp, several at a time, then bend back and snap off sharp, beaklike piece of shell just above tail. Remove shell and discard. Using sharp paring knife, make shallow incision along back of each shrimp, exposing black digestive vein. Extract black vein and discard. Rinse shrimp under cold running water, drain, and dry with paper towels; set aside.

6. Using stiff-bristled brush, scrub clams and mussels under cold running water; remove beards from mussels. Remove and discard any cracked or open shellfish. Rinse shellfish and set aside.

7. Rinse all fish under cold running water and dry thoroughly with paper towels. Cut into 1½-inch-wide strips; set aside.

8. In large nonaluminum sauté pan or deep nonaluminum skillet, heat olive oil over medium-high heat until hot but not smoking. Add onions and sauté, stirring occasionally, 5 minutes, or until lightly golden.

9. Meanwhile, wash parsley and pat dry with paper towels. Trim stem ends and discard. Mince enough parsley to measure 1 tablespoon; set aside. Reserve remaining parsley for another use. With your fingers, crumble saffron threads.

10. Add garlic, saffron, and white wine to onions, and stir, scraping up any browned bits that are clinging to bottom of pan.

11. Add clams and simmer, covered, 4 minutes.

12. Add mussels and simmer, covered, another 2 minutes.

13. Add shrimp, monkfish, bass, and shark, and simmer, uncovered, 3 minutes, or just until shrimp turn pink and fish flakes easily with a fork.

14. Remove and discard any unopened shellfish. With slotted spoon, transfer fish and remaining shellfish to serving dish, cover loosely with aluminum foil, and keep warm on stove top.

15. Add chopped tomatoes, and hot pepper sauce to taste to broth and bring to a boil over high heat. Boil 8 minutes, or until sauce is reduced slightly.

16. Reduce heat to medium, stir in cream, and continue to reduce sauce, stirring occasionally, 3 to 4 minutes, or until thick.

17. Add salt and pepper to taste. Pour sauce over fish and shellfish in serving bowl. Sprinkle with chopped parsley and serve immediately.

LEFTOVER SUGGESTION

Any leftover fish stew may be drained, put into a covered container, and chilled for a seafood salad the next day. For the salad, arrange the fish on a bed of lettuce and garnish it with halved hard-boiled eggs, tomatoes, chopped scallions, and capers; drizzle with a mild vinaigrette and serve with crusty bread.

Stevie Bass

MENU 1 (Right)
Pear and Lettuce Salad with Olives and Anchovies
Spanakopita
Baked Tomatoes

MENU 2
Moussaka
Green Beans with Fennel Seeds
Tomato and Cucumber Salad

MENU 3
Lamb Kabobs with Parslied Almond Rice
Greek Salad

When cooking for company, Stevie Bass likes to tantalize her guests with the unexpected and dramatic. She finds that serving ethnic food is a good way to please a crowd. Here, all three of her menus feature Greek main courses well known to Americans. Each menu balances color, flavor, and texture, and all are easy to prepare.

In Menu 1, the showstopper is *spanakopita*, or spinach pie, which here consists of layers of flaky filo pastry wrapped around a spinach and cheese filling. Although this dish may appear difficult, it is easy once you master handling the filo dough. With the spinach pie, Stevie Bass offers baked tomatoes with garlic, cheese, and oregano. The pear and lettuce salad can be served before, with, or after the main course.

Originally a Middle Eastern dish, the *moussaka* of Menu 2 has been adopted by the Greeks. The principal ingredient is eggplant, which is subtly flavored with cinnamon and red wine. Green beans sparked with fennel and a simple tomato and cucumber salad are the refreshing side dishes.

In Menu 3, a number of popular Greek seasonings—oregano, bay leaves, rosemary, and garlic—flavor the lamb kabobs. Parslied almond rice and a Greek salad that includes feta cheese and Kalamata olives are the traditional accompaniments.

For this festive Greek meal, offer the spanakopita, *tossed salad, and baked tomatoes on typical Mediterranean pottery, and add a bowl of assorted Greek olives, if you wish.*

36

Pear and Lettuce Salad with Olives and Anchovies
Spanakopita
Baked Tomatoes

The spinach filling for the *spanakopita* is wrapped in filo, a tissue-thin pastry that is sold frozen in sheets in half-pound or one-pound boxes. To prevent the sheets from cracking when you separate them, thaw the entire block of dough in the refrigerator overnight; then, shortly before you need them, set out seven sheets to thaw. Never refreeze the extra dough or the sheets may stick together; refrigerate it and use it within a week.

Because filo can dry out and crumble when overexposed to air, you should work quickly and keep the pastry sheets moist. Unroll the dough and lay the seven sheets, unseparated, on a damp kitchen towel; cover them with a second damp towel. Work with one sheet of dough at a time, leaving the rest covered. The butter you brush on the sheets helps to separate the layers, keeps them moist, and turns the pastry a golden brown as it bakes. Take care, though—too much butter will make the pastry soggy.

WHAT TO DRINK

These Greek dishes require an acidic white wine. Try either a French Muscadet or an Italian Pinot Grigio or Verdicchio, served well chilled.

SHOPPING LIST AND STAPLES

¾ pound fresh spinach
Medium-size head romaine lettuce
2 medium-size tomatoes (about 1¼ pounds total weight)
3 medium-size cloves garlic
1 lemon
Large ripe pear, preferably Bartlett
Small bunch fresh oregano, or 1½ teaspoons dried
Small bunch fresh basil, or 1 teaspoon dried
5 tablespoons unsalted butter
1 egg
8-ounce container ricotta cheese
¼ pound Parmesan cheese
6 ounces feta cheese
½-pound package frozen filo dough
⅓ cup good-quality olive oil, preferably extra-virgin
2 tablespoons red wine vinegar
11-ounce jar Kalamata or other Greek olives
2-ounce tin anchovy fillets
3 tablespoons all-purpose flour
Freshly grated nutmeg
Salt and freshly ground pepper

UTENSILS

Food processor or grater
Large heavy-gauge skillet
9-inch springform pan
8-inch square baking dish
Small heavy-gauge saucepan or butter warmer
Large bowl
Large strainer
Measuring cups and spoons
Chef's knife
Paring knife
Wooden spoon
Metal spatula
Rubber spatula
Pastry brush
Kitchen scissors
Small jar with tight-fitting lid

START-TO-FINISH STEPS

Twenty minutes ahead: Set out 7 sheets of filo dough for spanakopita recipe.

1. Peel and mince 3 cloves garlic for salad and tomatoes recipes. Using food processor fitted with steel blade, or grater, grate enough Parmesan to measure ⅓ cup for spanakopita recipe and ¼ cup for tomatoes recipe; reserve remainder for another use. Crumble feta for spanakopita recipe. Prepare fresh herbs if using, or crush dried herbs.
2. Follow spanakopita recipe steps 1 through 10.
3. Follow salad recipe steps 1 through 6.
4. Follow tomatoes recipe steps 1 and 2.
5. While tomatoes and spanakopita are baking, follow salad recipe step 7 and serve as first course.
6. Follow tomatoes recipe step 3, spanakopita recipe step 11, and serve.

RECIPES

Pear and Lettuce Salad with Olives and Anchovies

Medium-size head romaine lettuce
8 flat anchovy fillets
12 Kalamata or other Greek olives
1 lemon
Large ripe pear, preferably Bartlett

⅓ cup good-quality olive oil, preferably extra-virgin
2 tablespoons red wine vinegar
1 teaspoon minced garlic
1 tablespoon finely chopped fresh basil, or 1 teaspoon
    dried, crushed
¼ teaspoon freshly ground pepper

1. Wash and dry lettuce. Tear into bite-size pieces and place in serving bowl.
2. Rinse and dry anchovy fillets; add to bowl with lettuce.
3. Drain olives; add to lettuce and anchovies.
4. Squeeze enough lemon juice to measure 1 tablespoon; set aside. Reserve remaining lemon for another use.
5. Wash pear and dry with paper towel. Halve pear lengthwise; remove core and stem and discard. Cut each half lengthwise into 4 slices and place on plate. Sprinkle with lemon juice to prevent discoloration and turn to coat evenly with juice. Add pear slices to salad; set aside.
6. For dressing, combine oil, vinegar, garlic, basil, and pepper in small jar with tight-fitting lid and shake until well blended; set aside.
7. Just before serving, shake dressing to recombine and pour over salad.

Spanakopita

5 tablespoons unsalted butter
7 sheets frozen filo dough, thawed
¾ pound fresh spinach
6 ounces feta cheese, crumbled
1 cup ricotta cheese
⅓ cup freshly grated Parmesan cheese
3 tablespoons all-purpose flour
1 egg
1 tablespoon minced fresh oregano, or 1 teaspoon dried,
    crushed
¼ teaspoon salt
¼ teaspoon freshly ground pepper
Pinch of freshly grated nutmeg

1. Preheat oven to 400 degrees.
2. Melt butter in small heavy-gauge saucepan or butter warmer over low heat.
3. Meanwhile, butter bottom and sides of 9-inch spring-form pan; set aside.
4. Fit 1 sheet of filo dough into prepared pan, pressing it against sides and allowing it to overlap edge of pan. Brush filo lightly with melted butter. Repeat, one sheet at a time, with 3 more sheets, brushing each layer with butter before adding the next. Using scissors, trim filo so dough hangs over sides of pan only about 1½ inches. Place trimmings in bottom of pan, brush with butter, and set pan aside.
5. Wash spinach in several changes of cold water; do not dry. Remove tough stems and discard.
6. Place spinach in large heavy-gauge skillet and cook, stirring, over high heat 2 to 3 minutes, or until limp.
7. Turn spinach into large strainer, pressing with back of spoon to remove excess moisture. Coarsely chop spinach. You will have about ⅔ cup.
8. Combine spinach and remaining ingredients in large bowl, and stir with wooden spoon until blended. Turn mixture into filo-lined pan and smooth.
9. Fold overhanging filo layers over filling. Brush 1 of the remaining sheets of filo with butter and fold in half, buttered-side in. Place dough on top of filling, tucking edges under to roughly form a round; brush lightly with melted butter. Repeat with remaining 2 sheets of filo.
10. Bake spanakopita 40 minutes, or until golden.
11. Transfer spanakopita to serving platter and carefully remove sides of pan. To serve, cut into wedges.

Baked Tomatoes

2 medium-size tomatoes (about 1¼ pounds total weight)
2 teaspoons minced garlic
¼ cup freshly grated Parmesan cheese
1½ teaspoons minced fresh oregano, or ½ teaspoon dried,
    crushed

1. Wash and dry tomatoes. Core and halve crosswise. Cut thin slice from bottom of halves so they will rest flat.
2. Place tomato halves cut-sides up in 8-inch square baking dish and sprinkle each with garlic, Parmesan, and oregano. Cover pan with foil and bake in 400-degree oven 20 minutes, or until tomatoes are heated through.
3. Using spatula, transfer tomatoes to platter and serve.

———————————

ADDED TOUCH

This popular soup is known in Greece as *avgolemono*. It is a tangy blend of eggs and lemon juice.

Egg-Lemon Soup

4 tablespoons unsalted butter
2 lemons
¼ cup all-purpose flour
4 cups chicken stock
2 eggs
Salt

1. Melt butter in medium-size nonaluminum saucepan over medium heat.
2. While butter is melting, squeeze enough lemon juice to measure ¼ cup; set aside.
3. Add flour to melted butter and whisk until blended.
4. Whisking continuously, add chicken stock and whisk until blended and smooth. Cook over medium-high heat, stirring occasionally, just until mixture comes to a boil.
5. Meanwhile, separate eggs, placing yolks in small bowl and reserving whites for another use. Whisk yolks just until blended.
6. Whisking continuously, gradually add ¼ cup hot stock mixture to yolks and whisk until blended.
7. Whisk yolk mixture into remaining hot stock mixture and cook over medium-high heat, whisking continuously, about 2 minutes, or just until mixture returns to a boil.
8. Remove pan from heat. Add lemon juice, and salt to taste, and whisk until blended. Divide soup among 4 bowls and serve.

Moussaka
Green Beans with Fennel Seeds
Tomato and Cucumber Salad

An ample portion of moussaka *paired with fennel-flavored green beans and a light salad makes ideal summer fare.*

The *moussaka*, with its custardy topping, is an excellent company meal. Be sure the eggplant you choose has smooth dark-purple skin that is free of blemishes. It should be firm and feel heavy for its size, an indication that it is fresh and moist. A shriveled eggplant is old and probably bitter. Refrigerate the eggplant wrapped in a plastic bag, and use it within two or three days.

WHAT TO DRINK

A medium-bodied and fruity red wine, such as a young Dolcetto or Chianti from Italy, a French Côtes du Rhône, a young Spanish Rioja, or a California Zinfandel, would be the right choice for this meal.

SHOPPING LIST AND STAPLES

1 pound lean ground beef or lean ground lamb
1 eggplant (1 to 1¼ pounds)
1 pound fresh green beans
2 large or 3 small tomatoes (about 1¼ pounds total weight)
Medium-size cucumber
Medium-size onion
Small bunch scallions
2 medium-size cloves garlic
Small bunch fresh oregano, or ½ teaspoon dried
1 lemon
1 cup milk
1 stick plus 2 tablespoons unsalted butter
2 ounces Parmesan cheese
6-ounce can tomato paste
3 tablespoons good-quality olive oil, preferably extra-virgin
2 tablespoons all-purpose flour
1 teaspoon fennel seeds
½ teaspoon cinnamon
Salt
Freshly ground pepper
⅛ teaspoon whole peppercorns
⅓ cup dry red wine

UTENSILS

Food processor or grater
Large heavy-gauge skillet
Steamer unit or medium-size covered saucepan large enough to accommodate collapsible steamer
Collapsible vegetable steamer (if not using steamer unit)
Small heavy-gauge nonaluminum saucepan
15 x 10-inch baking pan
Shallow 2-quart casserole
Medium-size bowl
Small nonaluminum bowl
Colander
Measuring cups and spoons
Chef's knife
Paring knife
2 wooden spoons
Metal spatula
Whisk
Pastry brush
Mortar and pestle (optional)
Rolling pin (if not using mortar and pestle)

START-TO-FINISH STEPS

1. Follow salad recipe steps 1 through 7.
2. Follow moussaka recipe steps 1 through 11.
3. While moussaka is baking, follow green beans recipe steps 1 through 4.
4. Follow salad recipe step 8, green beans recipe step 5, moussaka recipe step 12, and serve.

RECIPES

Moussaka

1 stick unsalted butter
1 eggplant (1 to 1¼ pounds)
Medium-size onion
2 medium-size cloves garlic
2 ounces Parmesan cheese
1 pound lean ground beef or lean ground lamb
3 tablespoons tomato paste
⅓ cup dry red wine
½ teaspoon cinnamon
Salt
Freshly ground pepper
2 tablespoons all-purpose flour
1 cup milk

1. Preheat oven to 425 degrees.
2. In small heavy-gauge nonaluminum saucepan, melt 6 tablespoons butter over low heat.
3. Meanwhile, wash eggplant and dry with paper towels. Trim ends and discard. Halve eggplant lengthwise, then cut each half crosswise into ¼-inch-thick slices. Arrange slices in single layer in 15 x 10-inch baking pan and, working quickly, brush slices with half of melted butter. Turn slices and brush other sides with remaining melted butter. Bake 20 minutes.
4. Meanwhile, halve and peel onion. Mince enough onion to measure 1 cup; set aside.
5. Peel garlic and mince enough to measure 1½ to 2 teaspoons; set aside.
6. Using food processor fitted with steel blade, or grater, grate enough Parmesan cheese to measure ½ cup; set aside.
7. Heat large heavy-gauge skillet over medium-high heat. Add beef or lamb and onion and sauté, stirring and breaking up any lumps, 4 to 5 minutes, or until meat is browned.
8. Remove skillet from heat. Using metal spatula, scrape up any browned particles clinging to bottom of skillet and

stir to combine. Stir in garlic, tomato paste, red wine, cinnamon, and salt and pepper to taste; set mixture aside.

9. Melt remaining 2 tablespoons butter in small heavy-gauge nonaluminum saucepan over medium-low heat. Whisk in flour. Whisking continuously, gradually add milk and whisk until blended. Cook sauce, stirring, over medium heat 1 to 2 minutes, or until it thickens and comes to a boil.

10. Remove sauce from heat, add Parmesan, and stir until blended; set aside.

11. Remove baked eggplant from oven. Arrange enough eggplant slices in a single layer to cover bottom of shallow 2-quart casserole. Top with half of meat mixture. Add another layer of eggplant and remaining meat mixture. Top with remaining eggplant and pour cheese sauce over casserole. Bake moussaka, uncovered, 20 minutes, or until heated through.

12. Using metal spatula, divide moussaka among 4 dinner plates and serve.

Green Beans with Fennel Seeds

1 pound fresh green beans
1 teaspoon fennel seeds
2 tablespoons unsalted butter
Salt
Freshly ground pepper

1. Place beans in colander and rinse under cold running water. Trim ends and discard.

2. Bring 2 cups water to a boil over medium-high heat in steamer unit or in medium-size saucepan large enough to accommodate collapsible vegetable steamer. Add beans to steamer basket, cover pan, and steam about 8 minutes, or just until crisp-tender.

3. Meanwhile, using mortar and pestle, crush fennel seeds, or place seeds between 2 sheets of waxed paper and crush with rolling pin; set aside.

4. Cut butter into several small pieces; set aside.

5. Drain beans, remove steamer basket, if necessary, and return beans to pan. Add butter, crushed fennel seeds, and salt and pepper to taste, and toss to combine. Divide beans among 4 dinner plates and serve.

Tomato and Cucumber Salad

2 large or 3 small tomatoes (about 1¼ pounds total
   weight)
Medium-size cucumber
Small bunch scallions
1 lemon
Small bunch fresh oregano, or ½ teaspoon dried
⅛ teaspoon whole peppercorns
3 tablespoons good-quality olive oil, preferably extra-
   virgin

1. Wash tomatoes and dry with paper towels. Core tomatoes and cut lengthwise into wedges. Place wedges in medium-size bowl and set aside.

2. Wash cucumber and dry with paper towels. Trim ends and discard; do *not* peel. Using fork, score cucumber lengthwise. Cut cucumber crosswise into ⅛-inch-thick slices and add to bowl with tomatoes.

3. Wash scallions and dry with paper towels. Trim ends and discard. Cut enough scallions crosswise into ¼-inch-thick slices to measure ⅔ cup and add to tomatoes and cucumber. Cover bowl with plastic wrap and refrigerate until ready to serve.

4. Squeeze enough lemon juice to measure 1 tablespoon; set aside.

5. Wash fresh oregano, if using, and dry with paper towel. Chop enough to measure 1½ teaspoons, or crush dried oregano.

6. Crush peppercorns under flat blade of chef's knife.

7. Combine oil, lemon juice, oregano, and pepper in small nonaluminum bowl and whisk until blended; set aside.

8. Just before serving, whisk dressing to recombine. Pour dressing over vegetables and toss until evenly coated. Divide vegetables among 4 salad plates and serve.

ADDED TOUCH

For these light flaky cookies, finely chop the nuts in the container of a food processor fitted with a steel blade or in a blender.

Butter Crescents

2 sticks unsalted butter or margarine, at room
   temperature
1¼ cups confectioners' sugar
1 egg yolk
1 teaspoon almond extract
¼ teaspoon salt
2 cups all-purpose flour
1 cup finely chopped pecans, almonds,
   or walnuts

1. Preheat oven to 350 degrees.

2. Combine butter and 1 cup confectioners' sugar in large mixing bowl and cream together with wooden spoon until well blended and fluffy.

3. Add egg yolk, almond extract, and salt, and beat until blended.

4. Gradually add flour and chopped nuts, beating until they are totally incorporated and dough is formed. If necessary, knead dough until smooth.

5. Break off small handfuls of dough and roll between your palms into ½-inch-thick ropes.

6. Cut each rope into 2-inch lengths and shape into crescents, placing each crescent on ungreased baking sheet as you form it. You should have about 7 dozen.

7. Bake crescents 10 to 12 minutes, or until bottoms are light brown. Tops of cookies should remain pale.

8. Using wide metal spatula, transfer cookies to wire racks. Sift remaining confectioners' sugar over warm cookies and set aside to cool.

Lamb Kabobs with Parslied Almond Rice
Greek Salad

Arrange the lamb kabobs decoratively on a bed of almond-studded rice, and accompany the main course with a Greek salad.

When buying the lamb for this recipe, ask the butcher for cubes cut from the upper portion of the leg, where the meat is lean and free of gristle. Meat from the shank portion is too tough for this recipe. If your budget allows, purchase cubes cut from the loin, which is the tenderest part of the lamb. Marinate the lamb longer than 30 minutes, if possible.

To be sure the onion cooks through by the time the lamb is ready, do not skewer whole wedges; rather, pull the wedges apart into layers, then thread them on the skewers alternately with the lamb cubes.

Despite advance soaking, the bay leaves may char a bit during broiling. Threading the leaves between the meat and onions keeps them from blackening too much. Caution your family and guests against eating these sharp-edged leaves, which can cause intestinal damage if swallowed.

WHAT TO DRINK

An austere red shipper's Saint-Émilion from France, a California Merlot, or an Italian Barbera would be excellent with the lamb.

SHOPPING LIST AND STAPLES

1½ pounds lean boneless lamb, cut into 1-inch cubes
1 head Boston lettuce
Medium-size tomato
Medium-size green bell pepper
Small cucumber
2 medium-size onions (about 1 pound total weight), plus 1 small onion
Medium-size clove garlic
Small bunch fresh parsley
Small bunch fresh oregano, or 3 teaspoons dried
Small bunch fresh rosemary, or ¼ teaspoon dried
1 lemon
4 tablespoons unsalted butter
¼ pound feta or mozzarella cheese
7 tablespoons good-quality olive oil, preferably extra-virgin
¼ cup red wine vinegar
11-ounce jar Kalamata or other Greek olives
1 cup long-grain white rice
2½-ounce package whole almonds
2 teaspoons sugar
16 bay leaves
Salt
Freshly ground pepper
⅓ cup dry white wine

UTENSILS

Medium-size heavy-gauge saucepan with cover
Broiler pan with rack
Shallow baking pan, plus 1 additional if using bamboo skewers

Salad bowl
Large glass or ceramic bowl
Measuring cups and spoons
Chef's knife
Paring knife
Whisk
Basting brush
Small jar with tight-fitting lid
Eight 10- to 12-inch metal or bamboo skewers

START-TO-FINISH STEPS

One hour ahead: If using bamboo skewers for kabobs, place in shallow baking dish with enough cold water to cover and set aside to soak.

1. Wash parsley, and fresh oregano and rosemary if using. Trim stems and discard. Mince enough parsley to measure 2 tablespoons for rice recipe. Mince enough oregano to measure 1 tablespoon each for lamb and salad recipes. Mince enough rosemary to measure ½ teaspoon for lamb recipe. Reserve remaining herbs for another use.
2. Follow lamb recipe steps 1 through 6.
3. While lamb is marinating, follow rice recipe steps 1 and 2.
4. While nuts are toasting, follow salad recipe steps 1 through 3.
5. Follow rice recipe steps 3 and 4, and lamb recipe step 7.
6. While rice cooks, follow salad recipe steps 4 through 10.
7. Follow lamb recipe steps 8 and 9.
8. When lamb is nearly finished broiling, follow salad recipe step 11 and rice recipe steps 5 and 6.
9. Follow lamb recipe step 10 and serve with salad.

RECIPES

Lamb Kabobs with Parslied Almond Rice

Medium-size clove garlic
1 lemon
1 tablespoon minced fresh oregano, or 2 teaspoons dried
½ teaspoon minced fresh rosemary, or ¼ teaspoon dried
⅓ cup dry white wine
3 tablespoons good-quality olive oil, preferably extra-virgin
2 tablespoons red wine vinegar
¼ teaspoon salt
¼ teaspoon freshly ground pepper
1½ pounds lean boneless lamb, cut into 1-inch cubes
2 medium-size onions (about 1 pound total weight)
16 bay leaves
Parslied Almond Rice (see following recipe)

1. Peel garlic and mince enough to measure 1½ teaspoons; set aside.
2. Squeeze enough lemon juice to measure 2 tablespoons; set aside.
3. Crush dried oregano and rosemary, if using.
4. For marinade, combine lemon juice, wine, olive oil,

vinegar, garlic, oregano, rosemary, salt, and pepper in large glass or ceramic bowl and whisk until blended.

5. Trim any fat and gristle from lamb, if necessary, and pat lamb dry with paper towels.

6. Add lamb to marinade and set aside to marinate at least 30 minutes.

7. Preheat broiler.

8. Halve and peel onions. Cut lengthwise into wedges and separate wedges into sections of 2 or 3 layers each.

9. Rinse and dry skewers, if necessary. Thread skewers alternately with lamb, onions, and bay leaves and arrange skewers in single layer on broiler rack. Brush generously with remaining marinade and broil meat 3 inches from heating element, turning once, about 6 minutes for rare, 7 for medium-rare, or 8 for well done.

10. Remove kabobs from broiler and serve on bed of parslied almond rice.

Parslied Almond Rice

2½-ounce package whole almonds
1 cup long-grain white rice
¼ teaspoon salt
4 tablespoons unsalted butter
2 tablespoons minced fresh parsley

1. Preheat oven to 350 degrees.

2. Chop enough almonds to measure ¼ cup. Spread almonds in shallow baking pan and toast in oven, shaking pan occasionally to prevent scorching, 5 to 6 minutes, or until golden.

3. Remove almonds from oven and set aside to cool.

4. Combine rice with 2 cups water and salt in medium-size heavy-gauge saucepan and bring to a boil over medium-high heat. Cover pan, reduce heat to low, and simmer 25 minutes, or until rice is tender and water is absorbed.

5. Just before serving, cut butter into small pieces.

6. Remove rice from heat. Add almonds, butter, and parsley, and toss with fork to combine. Turn onto platter.

Greek Salad

1 head Boston lettuce
Small cucumber
Medium-size tomato
Medium-size green bell pepper
Small onion
¼ pound feta or mozzarella cheese
12 Kalamata or other Greek olives
1 tablespoon minced fresh oregano, or 1 teaspoon dried
¼ cup good-quality olive oil, preferably extra-virgin
2 tablespoons red wine vinegar
2 teaspoons sugar
½ teaspoon salt

1. Wash and dry lettuce. Remove and discard any bruised or discolored leaves. Line salad bowl with lettuce; set aside. Reserve remaining lettuce for another use.

2. Wash and dry cucumber; trim ends and discard. Cut enough cucumber crosswise into ⅛-inch-thick slices to measure 1 cup; set aside.

3. Wash and dry tomato. Core tomato and cut into wedges.

4. Wash and dry bell pepper. Core, seed, and derib; cut pepper crosswise into ¼-inch-thick rings; set aside.

5. Peel onion and cut enough crosswise into ⅛-inch-thick slices to measure ½ cup; set aside.

6. Cut cheese into ¼-inch-thick 1-inch squares; set aside.

7. Drain olives.

8. Crush dried oregano, if using.

9. Add cucumber slices, tomato wedges, bell pepper rings, onion slices, and olives to lettuce-lined bowl. Top with cheese and sprinkle with oregano. Cover bowl with plastic wrap and refrigerate until ready to serve.

10. Meanwhile, combine oil, vinegar, sugar, and salt in small jar with tight-fitting lid and shake until well blended; set aside.

11. Just before serving, shake dressing to recombine and pour over salad.

ADDED TOUCH

These buttery shortbread-type cookies are typically Greek and have a mild citrus-spice flavor. They may be frozen after baking, if desired.

Honey Rounds

2 sticks unsalted butter, at room temperature
½ cup granulated sugar
¼ cup honey
2 teaspoons freshly grated orange peel
1½ teaspoons vanilla extract
¼ pound almonds
2½ cups all-purpose flour
1 teaspoon baking powder
½ teaspoon baking soda
3 dozen whole cloves, approximately
¼ cup confectioners' sugar

1. Preheat oven to 350 degrees.

2. Combine butter and granulated sugar in large mixing bowl and cream together until well blended and fluffy.

3. Beat in honey, orange peel, and vanilla extract.

4. Grind enough almonds to measure 1 cup. When ground, almonds should have texture of coarse flour.

5. Combine almonds, flour, baking powder, and baking soda in medium-size bowl and stir with fork to blend.

6. Add dry ingredients to butter mixture, one half at a time, stirring after each addition until a smooth dough is formed.

7. Pinch off walnut-size pieces of dough and shape into balls. Place on ungreased cookie sheet and flatten into ¾-inch-thick 2-inch rounds. You will have about 3 dozen rounds.

8. Press clove into center of each round and bake 10 to 15 minutes, or until bottoms are golden. Tops should be pale.

9. Remove cookies from oven and sift confectioners' sugar over them. Using wide metal spatula, transfer to wire rack to cool.

Rowena M. Hubbard

After many years of cooking professionally—and sampling the cuisines of many countries—Rowena Hubbard has found the vibrant and aromatic foods of Morocco to be especially delicious. "I love well-seasoned food," she says, "and I admire the way Moroccan cooks know how to use spices so that the basic ingredients in a dish are not overpowered."

In her first menu, she presents *couscous*, an elaborate and spicy dish that is found throughout the Maghreb (a region that includes the northern parts of Morocco, Algeria, Tunisia, and Libya). Of Berber origin, *couscous* exists in as many versions as there are cooks. Although it can be made with grains such as millet and barley, it is most often prepared with *couscous* grains, for which the dish is named. In North Africa, a cook may spend several hours steaming and tenderizing *couscous* grains in a special two-tiered pot called a *couscousière*. Rowena Hubbard shortens this lengthy process by simmering the grains in chicken stock. The accompanying stewed lamb with vegetables, and fiery *harissa*, a sauce made of chilies, garlic, olive oil, and spices, should be spooned over the *couscous* grains.

Menu 2 contrasts spicy-sweet lamb and apricots with a cucumber-yogurt salad. (For information on making your own yogurt, see the box on page 10.) Both dishes are complemented by parslied rice. In the easy-to-prepare Menu 3, chicken breasts are baked with lemons, olives, and a typically Moroccan mixture of spices. With the chicken, the cook serves a flavorful zucchini and tomato salad and cracked-wheat pilaf.

This lavish meal is great for a party. The lamb and vegetable stew is spooned on top of the golden couscous *grains, then sparked with red-hot* harissa *sauce. Temper the spices with a refreshing orange and olive salad.*

47

Moroccan Couscous
Harissa
Orange and Olive Salad

Golden grains of *couscous*, made from finely ground semolina wheat, are sold in bulk in Middle Eastern markets and health food stores, or packaged in many supermarkets and specialty food shops. Avoid instant *couscous*; it is an inferior substitute for the real thing. Store any extra uncooked *couscous* in an airtight container in a cool dry place, where it will keep indefinitely.

The *harissa* recipe calls for tiny, very hot Mexican *pequín* chilies. Sold in some southwestern supermarkets, *pequíns* are commonly found in Mexican groceries. If you prefer, you can use red pepper flakes, or purchase ready-made *harissa* in sauce or paste form. *Harissa* should be stored in a tightly sealed container in the refrigerator.

WHAT TO DRINK

With this spicy main dish, you can choose from several beverage options: ice-cold beer, especially dark beer; a light red wine, such as chilled Beaujolais or California Gamay; a spicy white wine such as California or Alsace Gewürztraminer; or a lightly sweet German Riesling.

SHOPPING LIST AND STAPLES

2 pounds boneless leg of lamb, cut into 1-inch cubes
3 large zucchini (about 2¼ pounds total weight)
2 large ripe tomatoes (about 1½ pounds total weight)
2 medium-size yellow onions (about 1 pound total weight)
4 medium-size carrots (about ¾ pound total weight)
2 medium-size cloves garlic
Small bunch coriander (optional)
Small bunch parsley
3 large navel oranges (about 2 pounds total weight)
2 medium-size lemons
4 tablespoons unsalted butter
2 cups chicken stock, preferably homemade (see page 9), or canned (optional)
15½-ounce can chickpeas
4¾-ounce jar pimiento-stuffed olives
½ cup good-quality olive oil, approximately
1 pound medium-grain couscous
15-ounce box golden raisins
2 teaspoons dried pequín chilies, or 2 teaspoons dried red pepper flakes
2¼ teaspoons ground cumin
1 teaspoon caraway seeds (optional)
¼ teaspoon powdered saffron
½ teaspoon ground ginger
Salt and freshly ground black pepper

UTENSILS

Food processor (optional)
Large heavy-gauge nonaluminum skillet with cover
Medium-size saucepan with cover
Small saucepan
Large heatproof platter
Large heatproof serving bowl
Large bowl
Small bowl
Strainer
Measuring cups and spoons
Chef's knife
Paring knife
2 wooden spoons
Mortar and pestle (optional)

START-TO-FINISH STEPS

1. Follow Moroccan couscous recipe steps 1 through 5 and couscous grains recipe step 1.
2. While lamb cooks, follow salad recipe steps 1 through 4 and harissa recipe steps 1 through 3.
3. Follow couscous grains recipe steps 2 and 3.
4. Follow Moroccan couscous recipe step 6 and harissa recipe step 4.
5. Follow salad recipe step 5, couscous grains recipe step 4, Moroccan couscous recipe step 7, and serve with harissa.

RECIPES

Moroccan Couscous

2 pounds boneless leg of lamb, cut into 1-inch cubes
2 medium-size yellow onions (about 1 pound total weight)
3 large zucchini (about 2¼ pounds total weight)
4 medium-size carrots (about ¾ pound total weight)
15½-ounce can chickpeas
1 cup golden raisins
2 tablespoons unsalted butter
½ teaspoon ground ginger
½ teaspoon salt

½ teaspoon freshly ground black pepper
¼ teaspoon powdered saffron
2 large ripe tomatoes (about 1½ pounds total weight)
Small bunch parsley
Couscous Grains (see following recipe)

1. Preheat oven to 200 degrees. If butcher has not done so already, cut lamb into 1-inch cubes. Set aside.
2. Peel onions; cut into ½-inch-thick wedges. Wash and dry zucchini and trim ends. Wash, peel, and trim carrots. Using food processor fitted with medium slicing blade, or chef's knife, cut zucchini and carrots into ¼-inch-thick rounds. Rinse and drain chickpeas in strainer.
3. In large bowl, combine onions, zucchini, carrots, chickpeas, and raisins. Toss to mix well; set aside.
4. Melt butter in large heavy-gauge nonaluminum skillet over medium-high heat. Stir in ginger, salt, pepper, and saffron and cook until butter foams. Add lamb and cook, tossing to coat with seasonings, 2 to 3 minutes, or until browned.
5. Stir in vegetable mixture and ½ cup water. Cover, reduce heat to low, and simmer 20 to 25 minutes, or until lamb and vegetables are tender. Place large heatproof serving platter in oven to warm.
6. Wash tomatoes and dry with paper towels. Core tomatoes and chop coarsely. Wash and dry parsley. Trim stems and discard. Finely chop enough sprigs to measure ⅓ cup.
7. Fold tomatoes and parsley into lamb mixture and turn onto warmed serving platter. Serve with couscous grains. Or, if you prefer, serve the lamb and vegetables over the grains in serving bowl.

Couscous Grains

2 cups chicken stock (optional)
2 tablespoons unsalted butter
½ teaspoon salt
2 cups medium-grain couscous

1. Place large heatproof serving bowl in 200-degree oven to warm.
2. Combine stock or 2 cups water, butter, and salt in medium-size saucepan over high heat and bring to a boil.
3. When water boils, add couscous grains, stirring until grains are well moistened. Cover pan, remove from heat, and let grains stand for 5 minutes.
4. Turn couscous grains into warmed serving bowl.

Harissa

1 teaspoon caraway seeds (optional)
2 teaspoons dried pequín chilies or dried red pepper flakes
2 medium-size cloves garlic
3 tablespoons good-quality olive oil
2 teaspoons ground cumin
½ teaspoon salt

1. If using caraway seeds, grind seeds using mortar and pestle. Crush chilies, if using, in mortar with pestle or under flat blade of chef's knife. Crush and peel garlic.

2. Combine ground caraway seeds, crushed chilies and garlic, and remaining ingredients in small saucepan and sauté, stirring constantly, over medium-high heat, about 2 minutes, or until garlic is light brown.
3. Remove pan from heat and set harissa aside to cool.
4. Pour harissa into small serving bowl. You will have about ¼ cup.

Orange and Olive Salad

3 large navel oranges (about 2 pounds total weight)
2 medium-size lemons
Small bunch coriander (optional)
4¾-ounce jar pimiento-stuffed olives
¼ cup good-quality olive oil
¼ teaspoon ground cumin

1. Peel oranges, removing as much white pith as possible. Cut oranges crosswise into ½-inch-thick slices. Arrange slices in overlapping pattern on large serving platter.
2. Halve lemons and squeeze enough juice to measure ⅓ cup. Wash and dry coriander, if using. Reserving 4 sprigs for garnish, chop enough remaining coriander to measure 2 tablespoons. Drain olives and chop enough to measure ½ cup.
3. Combine chopped olives, olive oil, lemon juice, chopped coriander, and cumin in small bowl. Stir briefly and spoon sauce over oranges.
4. Cover oranges with plastic wrap and refrigerate until serving time.
5. Just before serving, garnish salad with coriander sprigs, if desired.

ADDED TOUCH

These pastries are popular throughout Morocco. You can assemble them ahead and freeze them until needed.

Gazelle Horns

8-ounce package almond paste (1 cup)
1 cup confectioners' sugar
1 tablespoon rose water
17¼-ounce package frozen puff pastry sheets, thawed

1. Preheat oven to 450 degrees. Using food processor or heavy-duty electric mixer, combine almond paste, sugar, and rose water and mix well.
2. Using about 2 tablespoons for each, roll almond paste mixture into twenty-four 4-inch logs.
3. Unfold pastry sheets and cover with damp towel. Cut 24 rectangles of pastry, each 1½ by 4½ inches.
4. Wrap one piece of pastry around each almond log. Brush water over long edges and ends of pastry, and press together to seal. Form each log into crescent shape.
5. Place horns on ungreased baking sheets and prick tops with fork.
6. Bake 10 minutes, or until horns are lightly browned.
7. Using metal spatula, transfer gazelle horns to wire rack to cool. Serve when cool.

Braised Lamb with Apricots
Parslied Rice
Cucumber Salad with Pickled Beets and Black Olives

Lamb with apricots and almonds, served with parslied rice and cucumbers, beets, and olives, will surely delight guests.

The lamb dish is a variation on a traditional Moroccan *tagine* (stew), which requires lengthy cooking because tough cuts of lamb are generally used. Here the cook uses round-bone lamb chops, which are tender and cook in less than an hour. This quick method retains all the flavors of the original dish with much less fuss.

Whole roasted salted almonds are added to the lamb dish toward the end of the cooking time. If you purchase whole natural almonds instead, roast them as follows: Spread the almonds in a single layer on a baking sheet. Place the sheet in a cold oven, then turn the oven to 350 degrees and bake 12 minutes, or until the almonds are golden. Remove the almonds from the oven, sprinkle with a teaspoon of salt, and allow them to cool. The nuts will continue to brown slightly as they cool.

The orange-flower water used to perfume the lamb is made by distilling orange blossoms. This fragrant water is sold in liquor stores, well-stocked supermarkets, and Middle Eastern and Indian markets. The dish can be made without orange-flower water; it will be slightly less authentic but no less delicious.

WHAT TO DRINK

The lamb and its accompaniments need a full-bodied red wine such as a Margaux or similar wine from one of the other Bordeaux communes.

SHOPPING LIST AND STAPLES

Four 1-inch-thick round-bone lamb chops
 (about 1½ pounds total weight)
4 medium-size cucumbers (about 2½ pounds total weight)
Large onion
2 large cloves garlic
Small bunch each mint, coriander, and parsley
½ pint plain yogurt
4 tablespoons unsalted butter
3 cups chicken stock, preferably homemade
 (see page 9), or canned
8¼-ounce jar sliced pickled beets
10-ounce jar salt-cured black olives
8-ounce jar honey

50

4-ounce bottle orange-flower water
1½ cups long-grain white rice
5 ounces whole roasted salted almonds
8-ounce package dried apricot halves
½ teaspoon ground ginger
½ teaspoon cinnamon
½ teaspoon powdered saffron
Salt and freshly ground pepper

UTENSILS

Food processor (optional)
Large deep heavy-gauge skillet with cover
Medium-size heavy-gauge saucepan with cover
Medium-size bowl
Strainer
Measuring cups and spoons
Chef's knife
Paring knife
2 wooden spoons
Grater (if not using food processor)
Metal tongs

START-TO-FINISH STEPS

1. Follow lamb recipe steps 1 through 5.
2. While lamb is cooking, follow salad recipe steps 1 through 3 and rice recipe steps 1 through 3.
3. Follow lamb recipe step 6 and rice recipe step 4.
4. Follow salad recipe step 4.
5. Follow rice recipe step 5, lamb recipe step 7, and serve with salad.

RECIPES

Braised Lamb with Apricots

Four 1-inch-thick round-bone lamb chops
    (about 1½ pounds total weight)
2 large cloves garlic
Large onion
2 tablespoons unsalted butter
½ teaspoon ground ginger
½ teaspoon cinnamon
½ teaspoon freshly ground pepper
⅛ teaspoon powdered saffron
1 cup dried apricot halves
1 cup whole roasted salted almonds
¼ cup honey
½ teaspoon orange-flower water

1. Pat lamb chops dry with paper towels.
2. Crush garlic under flat blade of chef's knife; remove and discard peels. Peel onion and cut into ½-inch wedges.
3. Melt butter over medium-high heat in large deep heavy-gauge skillet. Stir in garlic, ginger, cinnamon, pepper, and saffron, and cook 2 minutes.
4. Add lamb chops and turn to coat both sides with seasonings. Sauté about 3 minutes on one side, or until slightly

browned. Turn with tongs and sauté another 3 minutes, or until browned.
5. Add onion, apricots, and ¼ cup water. Cover skillet, reduce heat to low, and cook lamb mixture 25 minutes.
6. After 25 minutes, remove cover, turn chops over, and add almonds. Drizzle in honey and sprinkle with orange-flower water. Cook chops, uncovered, another 15 minutes, or until tender.
7. Place 1 chop on each dinner plate and top with onion, apricots, almonds, and any remaining cooking liquid.

Parslied Rice

2 tablespoons unsalted butter
1½ cups long-grain white rice
3 cups chicken stock
¼ teaspoon salt
Small bunch parsley

1. Melt butter over medium-high heat in medium-size heavy-gauge saucepan.
2. Add rice and stir to coat thoroughly with butter.
3. Add chicken stock and salt, cover pan, and reduce heat to low. Cook rice 20 to 25 minutes, or until stock is completely absorbed and rice is fluffy.
4. Wash and dry parsley. Trim stems and discard. Finely chop enough sprigs to measure ¼ cup; set aside.
5. Just before serving, add parsley to rice and toss until evenly distributed. Divide rice among 4 dinner plates and serve.

Cucumber Salad with Pickled Beets and Black Olives

4 medium-size cucumbers (about 2½ pounds total weight)
Small bunch mint
Small bunch coriander
¾ cup plain yogurt
½ teaspoon salt
8¼-ounce jar sliced pickled beets
¼ pound salt-cured black olives (about ⅔ cup)

1. Wash and dry cucumbers. Halve lengthwise and scoop out seeds using teaspoon; do not peel. Wash and dry mint and coriander; trim stems and discard. Reserving 4 mint sprigs for garnish, finely chop enough mint to measure ¼ cup. Finely chop enough coriander to measure ¼ cup. Set aside.
2. Using food processor fitted with medium shredding disk, or grater, shred cucumbers. You should have about 2 cups shredded cucumbers. Squeeze out excess liquid from cucumbers in double thickness of paper towels.
3. Combine chopped mint and coriander, yogurt, and salt in medium-size bowl. Add cucumbers and stir to coat with dressing. Set aside at room temperature until ready to serve.
4. Just before serving, drain beets in strainer and dry with paper towels. Divide cucumber mixture, pickled beets, and olives among 4 salad plates and garnish each plate with a mint sprig.

Spicy Chicken with Olives
Cracked-Wheat Pilaf
Zucchini and Tomato Salad with Almonds

The essence of Moroccan cooking is captured in the main-course chicken dish, with its intriguing blend of seasonings. The side dishes are a pilaf made with cracked wheat, and zucchini sticks with cherry tomatoes and slivered almonds.

This light chicken dish balances the contrasting flavors of green olives, lemon, and cinnamon. In Morocco, special lemons preserved in salt and their own juice would be used, but here salty olives, lemon juice, and lemon zest are substituted.

WHAT TO DRINK

Choose either a spicy Gewürztraminer from Alsace or California or an acidic Sauvignon Blanc from California, Italy, or the French Loire.

SHOPPING LIST AND STAPLES

4 large boneless chicken breasts, halved, with skin intact (about 2¼ pounds total weight)
6 small zucchini (about 2 pounds total weight)
1 pint cherry tomatoes
Small bunch scallions
3 large cloves garlic
Small bunch coriander
4 medium-size lemons
6 tablespoons unsalted butter
3½ cups chicken stock, preferably homemade (see page 9), or canned
6-ounce can pitted green olives
15½-ounce can chickpeas
½ cup mild olive oil
10 ounces cracked wheat
4-ounce bag slivered almonds
1 teaspoon ground ginger
½ teaspoon cinnamon
¼ teaspoon ground cumin
¼ teaspoon Cayenne pepper, approximately
Salt and freshly ground black pepper

UTENSILS

2 medium-size heavy-gauge saucepans with covers
Small nonaluminum saucepan
14 x 7 x 2-inch nonaluminum baking dish
Small baking sheet
Medium-size nonaluminum bowl
Colander
Large strainer
Measuring cups and spoons
Chef's knife

Paring knife
3 wooden spoons
Grater
Zester (optional)

START-TO-FINISH STEPS

1. Wash and dry lemons. Thinly slice 1 lemon for chicken recipe. Using zester or fine side of grater, grate enough zest from 1 lemon to measure 1 teaspoon for chicken recipe. Squeeze enough lemon juice to measure ¼ cup for chicken recipe and ⅓ cup for salad recipe.
2. Follow chicken recipe steps 1 through 7 and salad recipe steps 1 through 4.
3. Follow cracked-wheat recipe steps 1 through 3.
4. While cracked wheat cooks, follow chicken recipe step 8 and salad recipe steps 5 through 7.
5. Follow cracked-wheat recipe step 4, chicken recipe step 9, salad recipe step 8, and serve.

RECIPES

Spicy Chicken with Olives

3 large cloves garlic
4 large boneless chicken breasts, halved, with skin intact (about 2¼ pounds total weight)
4 tablespoons unsalted butter
1 teaspoon grated lemon zest
1 teaspoon ground ginger
½ teaspoon cinnamon
½ teaspoon freshly ground black pepper
⅛ teaspoon Cayenne pepper
6-ounce can pitted green olives
15½-ounce can chickpeas
Small bunch scallions
Small bunch coriander
¼ cup freshly squeezed lemon juice
1 lemon, thinly sliced
¼ cup mild olive oil

1. Preheat oven to 400 degrees. Crush garlic under flat blade of chef's knife; remove and discard peels. Set aside.
2. Wash and dry chicken breasts. If butcher has not done so already, halve breasts. Place breast halves, skin-side up, in 14 x 7 x 2-inch nonaluminum baking dish.
3. Melt butter over medium heat in small nonaluminum saucepan. Add lemon zest to butter. Stir in garlic, ginger, cinnamon, black pepper, and Cayenne pepper, and mix well. Drizzle sauce over chicken.
4. Bake chicken, uncovered, in lower half of oven 30 minutes.
5. Meanwhile, drain olives. Place chickpeas in large strainer, rinse under cold running water, and set aside to drain.
6. Wash and dry scallions and coriander. Trim ends and discard. Thinly slice enough scallions to measure ½ cup. Finely chop enough coriander to measure ¼ cup.
7. Combine lemon juice, lemon slices, scallions, coriander,

and olive oil in medium-size nonaluminum bowl. Add drained olives and chickpeas and stir to combine. Set aside, stirring occasionally.
8. After chicken has baked 30 minutes, reduce oven temperature to 350 degrees. Spoon olive mixture over chicken and bake another 15 minutes, or until juices run clear when chicken is pierced with a knife.
9. Transfer chicken to serving platter and top with olive mixture and pan juices.

Cracked-Wheat Pilaf

2 tablespoons unsalted butter
1½ cups cracked wheat
3½ cups chicken stock
Salt and freshly ground pepper

1. Melt butter over high heat in medium-size heavy-gauge saucepan.
2. Add cracked wheat and cook, stirring, about 1 minute, or until all kernels are coated and wheat is lightly toasted.
3. Add chicken stock, cover pan, and reduce heat to low. Cook cracked wheat 35 to 40 minutes, or until tender but still firm to the bite.
4. Add salt and pepper to taste and turn pilaf into large serving bowl.

Zucchini and Tomato Salad with Almonds

6 small zucchini (about 2 pounds total weight)
⅓ cup freshly squeezed lemon juice
¼ cup mild olive oil
¼ teaspoon ground cumin
¼ teaspoon freshly ground black pepper
¼ teaspoon salt
Dash of Cayenne pepper
¼ cup slivered almonds
1 pint cherry tomatoes

1. Wash and dry zucchini; trim but do not peel. Cut zucchini into ¼-inch-thick by 2-inch-long sticks.
2. Place zucchini sticks in medium-size heavy-gauge saucepan and add ⅓ cup water. Cover and cook over high heat 1 to 2 minutes, or until crisp-tender.
3. Turn zucchini into colander and drain well. Transfer zucchini to large serving bowl and toss with lemon juice, oil, cumin, black pepper, salt, and Cayenne.
4. Cover bowl with plastic wrap and refrigerate zucchini at least 30 minutes.
5. Spread almonds on small baking sheet and toast in 350-degree oven 5 to 7 minutes, or until golden, shaking pan occasionally to prevent scorching.
6. Meanwhile, wash and dry tomatoes. Remove stems, if necessary, and cut tomatoes in half; set aside.
7. Remove almonds from oven and turn out onto paper towels to cool briefly.
8. Just before serving, add tomatoes to zucchini and toss to combine. Sprinkle toasted almonds over salad and serve.

Silvana La Rocca

S ilvana La Rocca acquired her love of good cooking and fine dining as a child growing up in Italy. Her maternal grandmother taught her how to make fresh pasta; her mother introduced her to the diversity of Italian cooking; and her father taught her how to select the freshest ingredients at the market and prepare them simply in the Abruzzo style.

Although she now makes her home in California, Silvana La Rocca is still very much an advocate of Abruzzese cooking. She has selected menus that concentrate on the seafood, pasta, and fresh produce typical of that region. In Menu 1, salmon steaks are crowned with a pungent green herb sauce and served with sautéed *radicchio* and stuffed tomatoes. Menu 2 is more informal, with its main course of *penne* (quill-shaped pasta) mixed with shrimp, crabmeat, and scallops. Oven-baked zucchini and peppers and prosciutto-wrapped asparagus spears are the accompaniments.

Menu 3 is a highly spiced Abruzzese favorite called *coniglio arrabbiato,* or angry rabbit, because the pieces of rabbit are cooked with fiery red pepper flakes. As a refreshing counterpoint to the rabbit, the cook serves spinach with butter and lemon juice, and small white onions in a sweet-and-sour sauce.

Elegant tableware enhances this meal of salmon steaks with green herb sauce, tomato cups filled with minted peas, and radicchio *and garlic cloves sautéed in olive oil.*

Salmon with Green Sauce
Sautéed Radicchio
Stuffed Tomatoes

For the salmon recipe, select pink, sockeye, or Atlantic salmon, all of which have distinctively flavored, firm oily flesh that ranges in color from white to deep coral. Salmon is available fresh or frozen, whole or sliced into steaks. There is no substitute for salmon for this recipe.

Native to Italy's Veneto province, *radicchio* is a ruby-red chicory highly prized for its beautiful color. It has a slightly bitter taste and, because it is imported, is costly. Look for *radicchio* at quality supermarkets and green-grocers, or at Italian markets. If *radicchio* is unavailable, use four small heads of Belgian endive, halved lengthwise, and prepare them the same way.

WHAT TO DRINK

Choose a good-quality California Chardonnay or a French white Burgundy (such as a Chablis *premier cru*) for this fish dinner.

SHOPPING LIST AND STAPLES

Four ½-inch-thick salmon steaks (about 2 pounds total weight)
4 small or 2 medium-size heads radicchio (about 1 pound total weight)
4 large ripe plum tomatoes (about 1½ pounds total weight)
Small bunch scallions
9 medium-size cloves garlic
Small bunch fresh mint
Small bunch fresh Italian parsley
Small bunch fresh rosemary, or 1 teaspoon dried
Large lemon, plus 1 lemon (optional)
2 tablespoons unsalted butter
10-ounce package frozen peas
2-ounce tin flat anchovy fillets
2-ounce jar capers
1¼ cups good-quality olive oil
¼ cup balsamic vinegar
Salt and freshly ground black pepper

UTENSILS

Food processor or blender
Medium-size sauté pan
Large heavy-gauge skillet
Broiler pan with rack
Medium-size bowl
Small strainer
Measuring cups and spoons
Chef's knife
Paring knife
Wooden spoon
Wide metal spatula
Rubber spatula
Metal tongs
Melon baller or serrated teaspoon

START-TO-FINISH STEPS

Thirty minutes ahead: Set out frozen peas to thaw for tomatoes recipe.

1. Wash scallions, mint, parsley, and fresh rosemary if using, and pat dry with paper towels. Finely chop enough scallions to measure ½ cup for tomatoes recipe. Set aside 4 mint sprigs for garnish, if using, for salmon recipe, and coarsely chop enough mint to measure 1½ tablespoons for tomatoes recipe. Set aside 6 sprigs parsley for salmon recipe, and finely chop enough parsley to measure 1 table-spoon for tomatoes recipe. Set aside 1 sprig rosemary, if using, for salmon recipe.
2. Follow tomatoes recipe steps 1 through 3.
3. Follow salmon recipe steps 1 through 3.
4. Follow radicchio recipe step 1 and tomatoes recipe step 4.
5. Follow radicchio recipe steps 2 and 3.
6. Follow salmon recipe steps 4 and 5.
7. While salmon is broiling, follow tomatoes recipe step 5 and radicchio recipe step 4.
8. Follow salmon recipe step 6 and serve with tomatoes and radicchio.

RECIPES

Salmon with Green Sauce

1 sprig fresh rosemary, or 1 teaspoon dried
Medium-size clove garlic
Large lemon, plus 1 lemon for garnish (optional)
4 teaspoons capers
6 sprigs fresh Italian parsley
3 tablespoons good-quality olive oil
2 tablespoons unsalted butter
2 anchovy fillets

Salt and freshly ground black pepper
Four ½-inch-thick salmon steaks (about 2 pounds
    total weight)
4 sprigs fresh mint for garnish (optional)

1. Preheat broiler.
2. Remove rosemary leaves from stem and set aside. Crush garlic under flat blade of chef's knife; remove and discard peel. Halve large lemon and squeeze enough juice to measure ¼ cup. Cut four wedges from second lemon for garnish, if using; set aside. In small strainer, rinse capers under cold running water; drain.
3. For green sauce, in food processor fitted with steel blade or in blender, combine rosemary, garlic, lemon juice, capers, parsley, 2 tablespoons olive oil, butter, and anchovies. Process 30 seconds. Scrape down sides of container and process another 30 to 45 seconds, or until mixture is smooth and well blended. Add salt and pepper to taste; set aside.
4. Wash salmon steaks and dry with paper towels. Coat steaks on both sides with remaining tablespoon olive oil. Place steaks on rack in broiler pan.
5. Adjust broiler pan so that steaks are about 4 inches from heating element, and broil 3 to 4 minutes. Using wide metal spatula, turn steaks and broil another 4 minutes, or until salmon is slightly golden and just barely flakes when tested with point of knife.
6. Divide salmon steaks among 4 dinner plates and top with a generous tablespoonful of green sauce. Garnish each with a lemon wedge and mint sprig, if desired.

Sautéed Radicchio

4 small or 2 medium-size heads radicchio (about 1 pound
    total weight)
8 medium-size cloves garlic
½ cup good-quality olive oil
Salt and freshly ground black pepper

1. Core, wash, and dry radicchio. Discard any bruised or discolored leaves. Halve each head of radicchio lengthwise, if small; quarter if large. Set aside. Crush garlic under flat blade of chef's knife; remove and discard peels.
2. In large heavy-gauge skillet, heat olive oil over medium-high heat. Add garlic and sauté 1 to 2 minutes, or until light golden brown.
3. Add radicchio, and salt and pepper to taste. Cook 2 to 3 minutes, or until radicchio just begins to wilt. Using tongs, turn radicchio and cook other side 2 to 3 minutes, or until outside leaves are tender but still firm. Remove skillet from heat, cover, and set aside until ready to serve.
4. To serve, divide radicchio among 4 dinner plates and spoon olive oil and sautéed garlic over it.

Stuffed Tomatoes

4 large ripe plum tomatoes (about 1½ pounds
    total weight)
Salt
½ cup plus 1 tablespoon good-quality olive oil

10-ounce package frozen peas, thawed
¼ cup balsamic vinegar
Freshly ground black pepper
1 tablespoon finely chopped Italian parsley
1½ tablespoons coarsely chopped mint
½ cup finely chopped scallions

1. Wash and dry tomatoes.
2. Cut ½-inch-thick slice from top of each tomato. Turn tomatoes upside down and squeeze gently to remove seeds and juice. Using serrated teaspoon or melon baller, carefully scoop out remaining seeds and pulp. Sprinkle insides with salt and invert on paper towels to drain.
3. Meanwhile, heat 1 tablespoon olive oil in medium-size sauté pan over medium-low heat. Add peas and cook, tossing, 2 minutes, or until heated through; set aside.
4. In medium-size bowl, combine remaining ½ cup olive oil, balsamic vinegar, and salt and pepper to taste. Mix well with fork. Taste, and adjust seasonings. Add sautéed peas, parsley, mint, and scallions. Toss gently; set aside.
5. Just before serving, fill tomatoes with peas and divide tomatoes among 4 dinner plates.

ADDED TOUCH

Select very fresh berries for this simple dessert and glaze them quickly so the hot sugar syrup does not cook them.

Strawberries with Apricot Cream

2 pints fresh strawberries
4 tablespoons unsalted butter
½ cup light or dark brown sugar, firmly packed
1 teaspoon cinnamon
½ cup dry vermouth
1 cup heavy cream
4 tablespoons apricot preserves
2 tablespoons confectioners' sugar

1. Place medium-size bowl and beaters for whipping cream in freezer to chill.
2. Place strawberries in colander and rinse briefly under cold running water. Shake gently to drain well.
3. Hull strawberries and halve if large.
4. Melt butter in large sauté pan over medium heat. Add brown sugar and cinnamon and cook, stirring, about 2 minutes, or until sugar melts.
5. Add vermouth, increase heat to high, and cook 3 to 4 minutes, or until liquid is reduced by half. Reduce heat to low.
6. Add strawberries to hot liquid and toss gently to coat. Remove pan from heat and set aside for 15 minutes.
7. Meanwhile, remove bowl and beaters from freezer. Whip cream with electric mixer until soft peaks form.
8. Turn apricot preserves into small bowl and fold in 3 heaping tablespoons whipped cream. Gently fold apricot mixture into remaining whipped cream.
9. Divide apricot cream among individual dessert plates. Top with warm strawberries, sprinkle with confectioners' sugar, and serve.

57

Penne with Seafood
Asparagus with Prosciutto
Baked Zucchini and Peppers

Serve the main course of penne *and seafood with prosciutto-wrapped asparagus and baked zucchini and bell peppers.*

Select thick asparagus spears that are plump and green with compact tips; open, leafy tips are a sign of age. Before storing the asparagus, cut a small piece from the bottom of each spear, then stand the spears upright in a container of cold water in the refrigerator. They should stay fresh for several days. Prosciutto is an Italian-style dry-cured unsmoked ham, usually eaten raw. Top-quality prosciutto is deep pink, moist, and not overly salty. If it is not available, substitute Westphalian ham.

Zucchini is a favorite Italian vegetable because of its delicate taste and texture. The most flavorful zucchini are never more than an inch in diameter and should be firm to the touch, bright green, and glossy.

WHAT TO DRINK

A straightforward, crisp white wine, served well chilled, is the best match for these dishes. An Italian Soave, Verdicchio, or Lacryma Christi, or a French Muscadet or shipper's white Graves would all go well here.

SHOPPING LIST AND STAPLES

4 medium-thin slices prosciutto (about ¼ pound total weight)
½ pound fresh bay scallops
½ pound cooked crabmeat
¼ pound fresh tiny shrimp, cooked, peeled, and deveined, or 5-ounce package frozen
8 thick fresh asparagus spears (about ⅔ pound total weight)
4 medium-size zucchini (about 1¼ pounds total weight)
2 medium-size yellow bell peppers (about ¾ pound total weight)
Medium-size yellow onion
Small bunch fresh basil, or 1 teaspoon dried
6 tablespoons unsalted butter
3 ounces Parmesan cheese
14-ounce can imported Italian plum tomatoes
⅔ cup good-quality olive oil, approximately
1 pound imported dried penne
½ cup dried bread crumbs
1 teaspoon dried oregano
Salt
Freshly ground black pepper

UTENSILS

Food processor (optional)
Stockpot
Large heavy-gauge nonaluminum sauté pan
Steamer unit, or heavy-gauge saucepan large enough to accommodate collapsible steamer insert, with cover
Collapsible vegetable steamer
Two 9-inch square baking dishes
2 large bowls
Small bowl
Colander

Measuring cups and spoons
Chef's knife
Paring knife
2 wooden spoons
Metal spatula
Grater (if not using food processor)
Metal tongs

START-TO-FINISH STEPS

One hour ahead: Set out frozen shrimp, if using, to thaw for penne recipe.

Thirty minutes ahead: Set out butter to come to room temperature for asparagus recipe.

1. In food processor fitted with steel blade, or with grater, grate enough Parmesan to measure ½ cup for penne recipe and ¼ cup for asparagus recipe.
2. Follow asparagus recipe steps 1 through 5 and penne recipe step 1.
3. While water is coming to a boil, follow zucchini and peppers recipe steps 1 through 4.
4. While zucchini and peppers bake, follow penne recipe steps 2 through 7.
5. While penne and tomatoes cook, follow zucchini and peppers recipe step 5.
6. Follow asparagus recipe step 6.
7. Follow zucchini and peppers recipe step 6.
8. Follow penne recipe steps 8 and 9, asparagus recipe step 7, and serve with zucchini and peppers.

RECIPES

Penne with Seafood

Salt
Small bunch fresh basil, or 1 teaspoon dried
Medium-size yellow onion
14-ounce can imported Italian plum tomatoes
¼ pound fresh tiny shrimp, cooked, peeled, and deveined, or 5-ounce package frozen, thawed
½ pound fresh bay scallops (about 1 cup)
½ pound cooked crabmeat (about 1⅓ cups)
3 tablespoons good-quality olive oil
1 tablespoon unsalted butter
1 pound imported dried penne
Freshly ground black pepper
½ cup freshly grated Parmesan cheese

1. Bring 4 quarts water and 1 tablespoon salt to a boil in stockpot over high heat.
2. If using fresh basil, rinse and pat dry. Coarsely chop enough basil to measure 1 tablespoon.
3. Peel and coarsely chop onion. Reserving juice, turn tomatoes into small bowl. Using chef's knife, coarsely chop tomatoes; set aside.
4. Wash shrimp and scallops and pat dry with paper towels. Wash, pick over, and flake crabmeat, discarding any bits of shell or cartilage.

5. Heat oil and butter in large heavy-gauge nonaluminum sauté pan over medium heat 1 minute. Add onion and cook, stirring occasionally, 2 to 3 minutes, or until onion is pale golden.

6. Meanwhile, add penne to boiling water and cook 12 to 15 minutes, or just until *al dente.*

7. Add basil, tomatoes and their juice to onion, and stir to combine. Reduce heat to low and simmer 10 minutes.

8. Add shrimp, crabmeat, and scallops to tomatoes and season to taste with salt and pepper. Simmer, uncovered, another 2 to 3 minutes. Meanwhile, drain penne in colander and turn into large bowl.

9. Pour seafood sauce over penne and toss quickly to mix. Sprinkle penne with ¼ cup Parmesan and serve remaining Parmesan on the side.

Asparagus with Prosciutto

8 thick fresh asparagus spears (about ⅔ pound
   total weight)
4 medium-thin slices prosciutto (about ¼ pound
   total weight)
¼ cup freshly grated Parmesan cheese
Freshly ground black pepper
5 tablespoons unsalted butter, at room temperature

1. Preheat oven to 375 degrees.

2. Wash asparagus, trim off woody ends, and peel if desired.

3. Place about 1 inch of water in bottom of steamer unit or in heavy-gauge saucepan fitted with collapsible steamer. Add asparagus spears, cover, and steam over high heat 3 to 4 minutes, or until crisp-tender. Remove from heat and set aside to drain.

4. Meanwhile, lay out prosciutto slices and sprinkle each with 1 tablespoon Parmesan, and pepper to taste. Place 2 asparagus spears on each slice and roll up, leaving ends of asparagus exposed.

5. Coat bottom of 9-inch square baking dish with 1 tablespoon butter. Place asparagus bundles in dish and dot with remaining butter. Set aside at room temperature.

6. Just before serving, bake asparagus bundles 5 to 6 minutes, or just until heated through.

7. Remove from oven and, using tongs, transfer asparagus bundles to 4 dinner plates. Serve immediately.

Baked Zucchini and Peppers

4 medium-size zucchini (about 1¼ pounds total weight)
2 medium-size yellow bell peppers (about ¾ pound
   total weight)
½ cup dried bread crumbs
⅓ cup good-quality olive oil
1 teaspoon dried oregano
Salt and freshly ground black pepper

1. Wash zucchini and dry with paper towels; trim but do not peel. Cut enough zucchini crosswise into ⅓-inch-thick slices to measure about 6 cups.

2. Wash peppers and dry with paper towels. Halve, core, seed, and derib peppers. Cut peppers lengthwise into

¾-inch-wide strips.

3. Combine zucchini and peppers in large bowl. Add bread crumbs, olive oil, oregano, and salt and pepper to taste. Toss well to combine.

4. Turn vegetable mixture into 9-inch square baking dish and bake in 375-degree oven 15 minutes.

5. Remove vegetables from oven and set aside to cool.

6. Just before serving, toss vegetables with metal spatula, scraping bottom of dish to mix oil and juices with vegetables. Divide vegetables among 4 salad plates.

ADDED TOUCH

Italians love to cook and eat the bright-orange blossoms of the zucchini plant, which are delectable batter-dipped and fried. You can find squash blossoms for sale seasonally at quality greengrocers or Italian markets; they are highly perishable and should be refrigerated immediately and used as soon as possible. Do not buy those that are wilted.

Deep-Fried Zucchini Blossoms

16 zucchini blossoms
4 eggs, at room temperature
½ cup freshly grated Parmesan cheese
1 cup buttermilk, approximately
1¼ cups all-purpose flour
4 to 5 cups vegetable oil
Salt
Lemon wedges for garnish (optional)

1. Quickly but gently wash and dry zucchini blossoms.

2. Open blossoms and remove pistils.

3. In small bowl, beat 1 egg with fork until very well blended. Add grated Parmesan and stir with wooden spoon until smooth paste is formed. If mixture is too thick, add 1 tablespoon buttermilk.

4. Spoon equal amount of egg mixture into cavity of each blossom, gently pressing mixture down in blossoms.

5. For batter, in medium-size bowl, stir together flour and enough remaining buttermilk to make a smooth paste.

6. In large bowl, beat remaining eggs until well blended. Add batter to eggs and stir until mixture has consistency of thick cream. If too thick, add 1 to 2 teaspoons cold water.

7. Fill large heavy-gauge skillet three-quarters full with oil. Heat oil over very high heat until deep-fat thermometer registers 375 degrees. Line platter with double thickness of paper towels.

8. One at a time, quickly and carefully dip each blossom into batter.

9. Add 2 or 3 blossoms at a time to hot oil. Fry about 1 minute, or until blossoms are golden brown on one side. Turn and fry other side about 2 minutes.

10. When blossoms are golden brown and crisp on all sides, remove with slotted spoon and drain on paper towels. Sprinkle with salt while hot. Continue frying remaining blossoms in same manner. When all blossoms are cooked, arrange on serving dish, garnish with lemon wedges, if desired, and serve immediately.

Angry Rabbit
Spinach with Lemon and Butter
Sweet-and-Sour Onions

Spicy rabbit topped with capers and pepper strips, lemony spinach, and sweet-and-sour onions are a typical Abruzzo dinner.

Rabbit, a meat neglected by many Americans, is sold frozen in some supermarkets and fresh at many specialty butchers. Because rabbit flesh is lean and delicate, the cook sears the meat before roasting it to seal in the juices. You can substitute 2½ to 3 pounds of chicken legs and thighs, which are similar in flavor, and prepare them the same way.

WHAT TO DRINK

A full-bodied white wine with pronounced character tastes best with this menu. Try a Greco di Tufo or Gavi from Italy, a good California Chardonnay, or a white Châteauneuf-du-Pape from southern France.

SHOPPING LIST AND STAPLES

2½ to 3 pounds rabbit pieces
2 pounds fresh spinach
Medium-size red bell pepper
Medium-size yellow bell pepper, preferably, or
    green bell pepper
1 to 1½ pounds small white onions (12 to 18 onions)
3 medium-size cloves garlic
Large lemon, plus 1 lemon (optional)
2 sticks unsalted butter, approximately
6-ounce can frozen orange juice concentrate
2-ounce jar capers
½ cup good-quality olive oil, approximately

½ cup white wine vinegar
2 tablespoons honey
2 tablespoons sugar
1½ teaspoons hot red pepper flakes, approximately
1 bay leaf
Salt and freshly ground black pepper
1½ cups dry white wine

UTENSILS

2 large heavy-gauge nonaluminum skillets, 1 with cover
Medium-size heavy-gauge nonaluminum skillet
Large saucepan
17 x 11 x 2-inch heavy-gauge nonaluminum roasting pan
Large bowl
Small strainer
2 colanders
Measuring cups and spoons
Chef's knife
Paring knife
2 wooden spoons
Metal tongs

START-TO-FINISH STEPS

1. Follow onions recipe step 1 and spinach recipe step 1.
2. Follow rabbit recipe steps 1 through 4.
3. While rabbit browns, follow onions recipe step 2 and spinach recipe step 2.
4. While rabbit and spinach cook, follow onions recipe steps 3 through 5.
5. While onions cook, follow spinach recipe step 3 and rabbit recipe steps 5 through 8.
6. Follow onions recipe step 6 and spinach recipe steps 4 through 6.
7. Follow rabbit recipe step 9, spinach recipe step 7, onions recipe step 7, and serve.

RECIPES

Angry Rabbit

⅓ cup good-quality olive oil, approximately
2½ to 3 pounds rabbit pieces
3 medium-size cloves garlic
2 tablespoons capers
1½ cups dry white wine
Medium-size red bell pepper

Medium-size yellow bell pepper, preferably, or green bell pepper
Salt and freshly ground black pepper
1 to 1½ teaspoons hot red pepper flakes
1 lemon for garnish (optional)

1. Preheat oven to 400 degrees. Lightly oil 17 x 11 x 2-inch heavy-gauge nonaluminum roasting pan. Set aside.
2. Wash rabbit pieces and dry thoroughly with paper towels. Bruise and peel garlic. In small strainer rinse capers under cold running water; set aside to drain.
3. Heat ⅓ cup olive oil in large heavy-gauge nonaluminum skillet over medium-high heat. Add bruised garlic cloves and sauté about 2 minutes, or until rich golden brown. Remove garlic with tongs and discard.
4. Add rabbit pieces to skillet in single layer. Increase heat to high and cook on one side 3 to 4 minutes, or until golden brown. Turn rabbit with tongs and cook another 3 to 4 minutes, or until browned.
5. When rabbit is browned, add wine and cook, scraping up brown bits that cling to pan, 3 to 5 minutes, or until wine is reduced by half.
6. While sauce is reducing, wash and dry bell peppers. Halve peppers lengthwise; core, seed, and derib. Cut peppers lengthwise into ½-inch-wide strips; set aside.

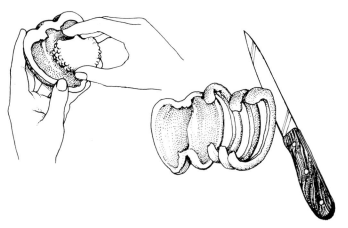

7. Reduce heat under rabbit to medium. Add salt, pepper, and hot pepper flakes to taste. Add capers and bell pepper strips, and stir to combine.
8. Remove skillet from heat and transfer rabbit, cooking liquid, and vegetables to prepared roasting pan. Place pan in oven, reduce heat to 375 degrees, and roast rabbit, uncovered, 20 minutes, or until juices run clear when meat is pierced with knife.

9. Just before serving, cut 8 thin wedges from lemon, if using for garnish. Divide rabbit pieces among 4 dinner plates and top with sauce, capers, and bell pepper strips. Garnish each plate with 2 lemon wedges, if desired.

Spinach with Lemon and Butter

2 pounds fresh spinach
Salt
1 stick plus 4 tablespoons unsalted butter, approximately
Large lemon
Freshly ground black pepper

1. In large bowl, wash spinach thoroughly in several changes of cold water. Remove stems and discard any leaves that are not crisp. Drain in colander; do *not* dry.
2. Place spinach in large heavy-gauge nonaluminum skillet and add a pinch of salt. Cook spinach, covered, over medium heat about 8 minutes, or until wilted.
3. Turn spinach into colander to drain and cool.
4. When cool to the touch, press down gently on spinach with back of spoon to remove excess water.
5. Heat 1 stick butter in same large heavy-gauge nonaluminum skillet over medium-high heat until butter begins to brown. While butter heats, halve lemon and squeeze enough juice to measure ¼ cup.
6. Add spinach, salt and pepper to taste, and lemon juice to skillet. Sauté spinach, tossing frequently, 4 to 5 minutes, or until spinach is heated through and well coated with butter; add more butter if desired.
7. Divide spinach among 4 dinner plates.

Sweet-and-Sour Onions

1 to 1½ pounds small white onions (12 to 18 onions)
3 tablespoons good-quality olive oil
3 tablespoons unsalted butter
1 bay leaf
2 tablespoons sugar
2 tablespoons honey
½ cup white wine vinegar
¼ cup frozen orange juice concentrate
Salt

1. Bring 3 quarts water to a boil in large saucepan over high heat.
2. When water boils, plunge onions into water and blanch 1 minute. Transfer onions to colander and place under cold running water until cool.

3. Carefully peel blanched onions and remove stems with paring knife. Dry onions thoroughly with paper towels.
4. Heat olive oil and butter in medium-size heavy-gauge nonaluminum skillet over medium-high heat. Add onions, bay leaf, sugar, honey, and vinegar, and stir to coat onions well.
5. Continue cooking, shaking pan from time to time, about 15 minutes, or until onions begin to turn golden.
6. Stir in orange juice concentrate, and salt to taste. Reduce heat to medium and cook onions, stirring occasionally, another 10 minutes, or until glossy and golden brown. Taste and add more salt if desired.
7. Divide onions among 4 dinner plates.

ADDED TOUCH

Tart, crisp apples are stuffed with an unusual mixture of *amaretti* (almond-flavored Italian cookies), blanched almonds, and hazelnut or almond liqueur.

Stuffed Apples

4 very firm cooking apples, such as McIntosh or Newtown Pippin (about 2 pounds total weight)
5 tablespoons unsalted butter, at room temperature
12 amaretti, crushed (about ⅓ cup)
2 tablespoons hazelnut or almond liqueur
¼ cup light or dark brown sugar, firmly packed
¼ cup blanched almonds

1. Preheat oven to 425 degrees.
2. Wash and dry apples. Remove stems and core apples, taking care not to cut all the way through bottom of apple.
3. In food processor fitted with steel blade, combine butter, amaretti, liqueur, brown sugar, and almonds, and process until smooth and pastelike.
4. Stuff mixture equally into cored apples. Using a fork, prick apple skins in several places.
5. Place apples, cored-end up, in small heatproof baking dish and pour ½ cup water around them.
6. Place in oven, reduce temperature to 400 degrees, and bake apples 30 to 40 minutes, or until medium-soft to the touch.
7. Remove baking dish from oven and let apples cool in pan.
8. When ready to serve, place apples on individual dessert plates. Serve at room temperature with pan juices drizzled over apples.

Georgia Downard

Although she was trained as a classical French cook, Georgia Downard has a particular passion for the earthy fare created in French country kitchens. She especially likes the robust, flavorful dishes of Languedoc and Provence, where, she says, "cooks make full use of the abundant fresh herbs, olive oil, tomatoes, and garlic indigenous to these areas." All three of her menus present French Mediterranean dishes seasoned with characteristic regional flair.

Menu 1 is a simple yet elegant dinner reminiscent of the cooking of Nice. It features seafood salad dressed with *aïoli* sauce, a heady garlic mayonnaise nicknamed "the butter of Provence." With the salad, the cook serves *tapénade* (sometimes referred to as Niçoise caviar), which is a combination of anchovies, black olives, capers, and olive oil, here spread on croutons and garnished with chopped hard-boiled eggs.

Menu 2 reflects the flavors of Languedoc, a region known for its fine game and abundance of fresh vegetables and fruits. For this meal, duck is braised with a ratatouille-like mixture of eggplant, zucchini, tomato, red bell pepper, and onion, and accompanied by a traditional rice pilaf flavored with saffron, and stuffed mushrooms with snail butter. Although the butter contains no snails, it is so called because it is always used to fill *escargots à la bourguignonne*.

In Menu 3, loin lamb chops are enhanced with rosemary, thyme, savory, and basil, then sautéed with garlic and topped with a rich Roquefort sauce. With the chops, Georgia Downard presents a crispy potato cake and zucchini tossed with *pistou*, Provence's version of Genoese *pesto* sauce.

Painted ceramic tiles establish a country French mood for this Provençal meal of tapénade *spread on croutons and a carefully composed seafood salad with vegetables and Niçoise olives.*

65

Tapénade Toasts
Seafood Salad à la Niçoise

For this lovely summer menu, let the marketplace and your personal preferences dictate what seafood you use in the salad: Mussels, lobster meat, or a firm-fleshed white fish such as halibut are good substitutes for the shrimp or scallops. To save time, you can cook the seafood in the morning and refrigerate it until dinnertime. Don't dress it with the *aïoli* until just before serving, however, or the seafood will absorb too much of the dressing and will change in texture. Accompany the seafood salad with whatever colorful vegetables you wish.

WHAT TO DRINK

The cook recommends a well-chilled dry white wine to complement this menu. A Muscadet would go well, as would a Sancerre or Pouilly-Fumé.

SHOPPING LIST AND STAPLES

¾ pound large shrimp
¾ pound sea scallops
½ pound squid, cleaned
1 pound small new potatoes
¾ pound green beans
2 medium-size tomatoes (about 1 pound total weight)
3 large cloves plus 1 medium-size clove garlic
Small bunch each thyme, rosemary, and parsley
2 lemons
4 eggs
½ pint sour cream
4 tablespoons unsalted butter
2-ounce tin flat anchovy fillets
12 ounces black olives, preferably oil-cured or Kalamata
3½-ounce jar imported capers
1¾ cups good-quality olive oil, approximately
1 tablespoon tarragon vinegar
2 teaspoons Dijon mustard
1 long loaf French bread (baguette)
Salt and freshly ground pepper

UTENSILS

Food processor or blender
Large saucepan with cover
Medium-size saucepan
Small saucepan
15 x 10-inch baking sheet
3 large bowls, 1 nonaluminum
2 small bowls
Colander
Small strainer
Measuring cups and spoons
Chef's knife
Paring knife
Serrated bread knife
Wooden spoon
Slotted spoon
Rubber spatula
Whisk
Vegetable brush

START-TO-FINISH STEPS

One hour ahead: Set out eggs to come to room temperature for toasts and salad recipes.

1. Squeeze enough lemon juice to measure 1 tablespoon for toasts recipe and about 4 tablespoons for salad recipe. Peel garlic for toasts and salad recipes.
2. Follow toasts recipe steps 1 through 3.
3. Follow salad recipe steps 1 through 6 and toasts recipe steps 4 through 7.
4. Follow salad recipe steps 7 through 10.
5. Follow toasts recipe step 8 and salad recipe steps 11 and 12.
6. Follow toasts recipe steps 9 and 10.
7. Follow salad recipe steps 13 through 16 and serve with toasts.

RECIPES

Tapénade Toasts

4 tablespoons unsalted butter
2-ounce tin flat anchovy fillets
2 tablespoons imported capers
Small bunch parsley
Small bunch thyme
Small bunch rosemary
1 cup black olives, preferably oil-cured or Kalamata, pitted
Medium-size clove garlic, peeled
1 tablespoon freshly squeezed lemon juice

3 to 4 tablespoons good-quality olive oil
Freshly ground pepper
2 eggs, at room temperature
1 long loaf French bread (baguette)

1. Preheat oven to 400 degrees. Set out butter to come to room temperature.
2. Drain anchovies and pat dry with paper towels. Rinse capers in small strainer under cold running water and drain. Wash herbs and pat dry. Set aside 12 sprigs parsley for garnish. Mince enough thyme and rosemary to measure ¾ teaspoon each; set aside.
3. In food processor or blender, combine anchovies, capers, thyme, rosemary, olives, garlic, and lemon juice. Process until smooth. With motor running, gradually add 3 tablespoons oil, or enough to just hold spread together. Transfer tapénade to small bowl and add pepper to taste.
4. In small saucepan, bring 2 cups water to a simmer.
5. Place eggs in simmering water and cook 8 to 10 minutes, or until hard-boiled.
6. Meanwhile, cut bread into twelve ½-inch-thick slices with serrated knife. Butter slices on one side and arrange, buttered-side up, on baking sheet.
7. Drain eggs and cool under cold running water.
8. Toast bread in oven 7 to 10 minutes, or until golden.
9. Peel eggs and chop finely.
10. Spread toasts with tapénade. Sprinkle chopped egg around edges and garnish each toast with a sprig of parsley. Arrange toasts decoratively on platter and set aside until ready to serve.

Seafood Salad à la Niçoise

¾ pound large shrimp
1 pound small new potatoes
Salt
¾ pound green beans
½ pound squid, cleaned
¾ pound sea scallops
2 eggs, at room temperature
3 large cloves garlic, peeled
4 tablespoons freshly squeezed lemon juice,
    approximately
Freshly ground pepper
1½ cups good-quality olive oil
3 tablespoons sour cream
2 medium-size tomatoes (about 1 pound total weight)
1 tablespoon tarragon vinegar
2 teaspoons Dijon mustard
½ cup black olives, preferably oil-cured or
    Kalamata, pitted

1. Peel and devein shrimp: Pinch off legs of shrimp, several at a time, then bend back and snap off sharp, beaklike piece of shell just above tail. Remove shell, except for tail, and discard. Using sharp paring knife, make shallow incision along back of each shrimp, exposing digestive vein. Extract vein and discard. Place shrimp in colander, rinse under cold running water, and drain.

Pinch off legs to remove shell.
    Extract black digestive vein with your fingers.

2. Scrub potatoes under cold running water and place in large saucepan. Add cold water to cover by 2 inches and ½ teaspoon salt. Partially cover pan, bring water to a boil over high heat, and simmer 15 to 20 minutes, or until potatoes are tender when pierced with tip of paring knife.
3. Meanwhile, bring 1 quart water and ½ teaspoon salt to a boil in medium-size saucepan over high heat.
4. Wash and drain green beans. Trim ends and discard.
5. Rinse squid under cold running water. Cut off tentacles and cut into bite-size pieces. Cut body sac into ¼-inch-wide rings. Place scallops in colander and rinse under cold running water. Halve scallops if very large.
6. Add shrimp and scallops to boiling water and cook over medium-high heat, stirring, 2 minutes. Add squid and cook 1 to 2 minutes more, or until seafood is opaque and just firm. Drain seafood in colander; transfer to large bowl and set aside to cool.
7. When cooked, transfer potatoes to colander with slotted spoon and refresh under cold running water. Set aside to cool. Keep water in saucepan at a boil.
8. Add beans to boiling water, reduce heat to medium, cover, and cook 5 minutes, or just until crisp-tender.
9. Meanwhile, separate 1 egg, placing yolk in small bowl and reserving white for another use.
10. Turn beans into colander and refresh under cold running water. Drain and set aside to cool.
11. For aïoli, in food processor or blender, combine egg yolk, whole egg, garlic, 2 tablespoons lemon juice, and salt and pepper to taste. Process until smooth. With motor running add 1 cup olive oil in a slow, steady stream. Add sour cream, and process briefly to combine. Adjust seasoning, adding a little lemon juice, salt, and pepper to taste.
12. Transfer aïoli to large bowl. Using slotted spoon, add seafood, and toss gently to coat.
13. Wash and dry tomatoes. Core tomatoes and cut into wedges.
14. Peel potatoes and cut into ¼-inch-thick slices.
15. For vinaigrette, in large nonaluminum bowl, combine 1 tablespoon lemon juice, vinegar, mustard, and salt and pepper to taste. Whisking continuously, gradually add remaining ½ cup olive oil and whisk until blended.
16. Divide seafood among 4 dinner plates and surround with beans, tomato wedges, and sliced potatoes; scatter olives on top. Drizzle vegetables with vinaigrette and serve.

Stuffed Mushrooms with Snail Butter
Braised Duck and Vegetables
Saffron Pilaf

Stuffed mushroom caps with snail butter can be served with or before the main course of braised duck and vegetables flavored with garlic and herbs. A side dish of saffron rice provides a handsome color contrast.

Stuffed mushroom caps are a delicious offering any time of the year. Choose large white mushrooms with smooth unmottled skins, and wipe the mushrooms clean with a damp paper towel; soaking makes them soggy. For a fuller flavor, begin marinating the mushrooms early in the day. To mop up the garlicky butter, the cook suggests serving crusty Italian bread as an accompaniment.

Ducks raised in America are often quite fatty. Remove as much excess fat as possible from under the skin, then prick the skin well to release the remaining fat during cooking. Because the duck is quartered, it cooks through within an hour. This one-pot entrée can be prepared in the morning and reheated at dinnertime, or, if possible, let it sit for a day in the refrigerator for an even richer taste.

WHAT TO DRINK

The full flavors of these dishes demand a robust wine with character. A top-quality Rhône wine, such as Châteauneuf-du-Pape or Hermitage, would be superb here; an Italian Barolo or a top-quality California Zinfandel is a good second choice.

SHOPPING LIST AND STAPLES

4- to 4½-pound whole duck
16 large mushrooms (about 1 pound total weight)
Medium-size eggplant (about 1 pound)
2 medium-size zucchini (about 1 pound total weight)
Medium-size red bell pepper
3 medium-size onions (about 1 pound total weight)
4 large cloves garlic
Large bunch parsley
Small bunch each rosemary, basil, thyme, and tarragon
Small orange
1 lemon
1 stick plus 4 tablespoons unsalted butter
2 ounces Gruyère cheese
2 ounces Parmesan cheese, preferably imported
2¼ cups chicken stock, preferably homemade (see page 9), or canned
2-ounce jar imported capers
16-ounce can imported plum tomatoes
6-ounce can tomato paste
⅓ cup good-quality olive oil, approximately
1 teaspoon Dijon mustard
1½ cups long-grain white rice

3 tablespoons dried bread crumbs
2 bay leaves
⅛ teaspoon powdered saffron
Salt
Freshly ground pepper
½ cup dry white wine

5. Follow pilaf recipe steps 1 through 6 and mushrooms recipe step 11.
6. Follow duck recipe step 11.
7. Follow pilaf recipe step 7, mushrooms recipe step 12, and serve with duck.

UTENSILS

Food processor or blender
Large heavy-gauge sauté pan with cover
Large heavy-gauge skillet
Medium-size ovenproof saucepan with cover
Large gratin dish
Large nonaluminum bowl
Small bowl
Small strainer
Measuring cups and spoons
Cleaver
Chef's knife
Paring knife
2 wooden spoons
Grater (if not using food processor)
Citrus juicer (optional)
Metal tongs
Cheesecloth
Kitchen string

START-TO-FINISH STEPS

1. Wash fresh herbs and pat dry. Set aside 13 sprigs parsley for pilaf recipe and mince enough remaining parsley to measure 6 tablespoons for mushrooms recipe. Mince enough thyme to measure 3 teaspoons for duck recipe, 1½ teaspoons for pilaf recipe, and ½ teaspoon for mushrooms recipe. Mince enough tarragon to measure ½ teaspoon for mushrooms recipe and enough basil and rosemary to measure 3 teaspoons each for duck recipe. Peel garlic and mince 1 clove for mushrooms recipe and 3 cloves for duck recipe. Halve and peel onions. Coarsely chop enough onion to measure 1 cup for duck recipe. Mince enough onion to measure 1 cup for pilaf recipe and ⅓ cup for mushrooms recipe.
2. Follow mushrooms recipe steps 1 through 6.
3. Follow duck recipe steps 1 through 10.
4. While duck is cooking, follow mushrooms recipe steps 7 through 10.

RECIPES

Stuffed Mushrooms with Snail Butter

1 stick unsalted butter
1 lemon
2 ounces Gruyère cheese
2 ounces Parmesan cheese, preferably imported
16 large mushrooms (about 1 pound total weight)
¼ cup good-quality olive oil, approximately
Salt and freshly ground pepper
⅓ cup minced onion
½ teaspoon minced thyme
½ teaspoon minced tarragon
3 tablespoons dried bread crumbs
6 tablespoons minced parsley
1 large clove garlic, minced
1 teaspoon Dijon mustard

1. Preheat oven to 350 degrees. Set out butter to come to room temperature. Oil large gratin dish and set aside.
2. Squeeze enough lemon juice to measure 4 teaspoons; set aside.
3. In food processor fitted with steel blade, or with grater, grate enough Gruyère and Parmesan to measure 3 tablespoons each. Reserve remaining cheese for another use.
4. Wipe mushrooms clean with damp paper towels. Remove stems and set stems aside.
5. Combine 2 teaspoons lemon juice, 2 tablespoons olive oil, and salt and pepper to taste in large nonaluminum bowl. Add mushroom caps and toss to coat; set aside.
6. Coarsely chop mushroom stems and squeeze in paper towels to extract excess moisture; set aside.
7. In large heavy-gauge skillet, heat 2 tablespoons butter and remaining olive oil over medium-high heat. When foam subsides, add onion and cook, stirring, 1 minute. Add mushroom stems, thyme, tarragon, and salt and pepper to taste, and cook, stirring, 3 to 4 minutes, or until liquid has almost completely evaporated. Remove skillet from heat and stir in Gruyère, Parmesan, bread crumbs, and 3 tablespoons minced parsley. Taste, and adjust seasonings if necessary.

8. Arrange mushroom caps, gill-sides up, in gratin dish and stuff each cap with cheese mixture.

9. For snail butter, in small bowl, combine remaining butter, parsley, and lemon juice, minced garlic, mustard, and salt and pepper to taste.

10. Dot stuffed mushrooms with snail butter.

11. Bake mushrooms 20 minutes, or until tops are golden.

12. Transfer mushrooms to platter and serve.

Braised Duck and Vegetables

Small orange
2 tablespoons imported capers
4- to 4½-pound whole duck
Salt and freshly ground pepper
1 tablespoon good-quality olive oil
Medium-size eggplant (about 1 pound)
2 medium-size zucchini (about 1 pound total weight)
Medium-size red bell pepper
1 cup coarsely chopped onion
16-ounce can imported plum tomatoes
½ cup dry white wine
1 tablespoon tomato paste
3 large cloves garlic, minced
3 teaspoons each minced thyme, rosemary, and basil
1 bay leaf

1. Wash orange. Using sharp paring knife, cut off two 3-inch by 1-inch strips of rind, avoiding white pith as much as possible. Reserve orange for another use.

2. Rinse capers in strainer under cold water and drain.

3. Remove and discard any excess fat from cavity of duck. Trim and discard neck skin. Chop off wing tips and reserve with neck and giblets for another use. Using cleaver, quarter duck: Turn duck breast-side up on cutting surface and cut through breastbone. Turn duck over, push back breast halves, and cut backbone in two. Next, feeling for end of rib cage, cut pieces in half just below ribs. Using sharp knife, trim excess skin and any visible fat from each quarter. Prick skin all over with tip of paring knife. Season duck with salt and pepper; set aside.

4. In large heavy-gauge sauté pan, heat olive oil over medium heat. When oil is hot, add duck and cook 4 minutes on each side, or until browned.

5. Meanwhile, wash and dry eggplant, zucchini, and bell pepper. Trim but do not peel eggplant; cut into 1-inch cubes. Trim but do not peel zucchini; cut into ½-inch-thick slices. Halve, core, seed, and coarsely chop pepper.

6. Using tongs, transfer duck to large plate and pour off all but 2 tablespoons fat from pan.

7. Add onion to fat in pan and cook over medium-high heat, stirring occasionally, until onion is softened. Add eggplant, zucchini, and bell pepper, and cook, stirring occasionally, 3 more minutes.

8. Meanwhile, in food processor or blender, purée tomatoes with their juice.

9. Add wine to pan and boil mixture 1 minute.

10. Return duck pieces to pan, spooning vegetables over and around them. Add orange rind, tomato purée, tomato paste, garlic, thyme, rosemary, basil, and bay leaf. Bring liquid to a boil, reduce heat to medium, and cover pan. Braise duck and vegetables, stirring occasionally and skimming fat, 40 minutes, or until duck is tender.

11. Remove pan from heat; discard bay leaf and orange rind. Skim any remaining fat from surface. Stir in capers, and add salt and pepper to taste. Transfer duck to large serving dish and top with vegetables.

Saffron Pilaf

4 tablespoons unsalted butter, approximately
12 sprigs parsley, plus 1 sprig for garnish
1½ teaspoons minced thyme
1 bay leaf
1 cup minced onion
1½ cups long-grain white rice
2¼ cups chicken stock
⅛ teaspoon powdered saffron
Salt

1. Cut out waxed-paper disk slightly smaller than diameter of medium-size ovenproof saucepan; butter one side.

2. For bouquet garni, combine 12 sprigs parsley, thyme, and bay leaf in small piece of cheesecloth and tie with kitchen string.

3. In medium-size ovenproof saucepan, melt 4 tablespoons butter over medium heat. Add onion and cook 2 minutes, stirring occasionally, or until onion is softened.

4. Add rice and cook, stirring, 2 more minutes.

5. Add bouquet garni, stock, saffron, and salt to taste, and stir to combine. Bring liquid to a boil, stirring occasionally. Remove pan from heat and cover mixture with buttered waxed paper and the pan cover.

6. Bake rice in 350-degree oven 18 minutes, or until tender.

7. Discard bouquet garni. Transfer pilaf to serving dish and garnish with sprig of parsley.

Lamb Chops with Fresh Herbs, Garlic, and Roquefort Sauce
Zucchini Noodles with Pistou Sauce
Potato Cake

A good red wine complements lamb chops with Roquefort sauce, zucchini with pistou, and a crispy golden potato cake.

Sautéing an entire head of garlic with the lamb may seem overpowering, but the preliminary simmering of the unpeeled cloves tames their pungency. For an even milder taste and a buttery consistency, simmer the garlic for a full 15 minutes. When sautéing the garlic, take care not to burn it, or it will turn bitter.

WHAT TO DRINK

If you are feeling experimental, you might try a well-aged red wine from Spain's Rioja region or a vintage Côtes du Rhône with this menu. Otherwise, select a good California Zinfandel or Italian Barolo.

SHOPPING LIST AND STAPLES

Four ½- to ¾-inch-thick loin lamb chops (about 1¼ pounds total weight)
4 small zucchini (about 1½ pounds total weight)
2 plum tomatoes (about ½ pound total weight)
1½ pounds all-purpose potatoes
1 shallot
18 cloves garlic
Large bunch basil
Small bunch each rosemary, thyme, savory, and parsley
1 lemon
1 pint heavy cream
1 stick plus 5 tablespoons unsalted butter
2 ounces Roquefort cheese
2 ounces Parmesan cheese, preferably imported
7-ounce jar Niçoise or other small imported black olives
⅔ cup good-quality olive oil, approximately
3-ounce can walnut pieces
⅛ teaspoon nutmeg
Cayenne pepper
Salt and freshly ground pepper
¾ cup dry white wine

UTENSILS

Food processor or blender
Large skillet
Medium-size heavy-gauge nonaluminum skillet with cover
10-inch nonstick skillet
Medium-size saucepan with cover
Small heavy-gauge nonaluminum saucepan
2 heatproof serving platters
Medium-size bowl
3 small bowls
Colander
Strainer
Measuring cups and spoons
Chef's knife
Paring knife
2 large metal spatulas
2 wooden spoons
Rubber spatula

Metal tongs
Grater (if not using food processor)
Vegetable peeler

START-TO-FINISH STEPS

1. Wash herbs and pat dry with paper towels. Set aside 1 cup firmly packed basil leaves for zucchini recipe. For lamb chops recipe, set aside 10 to 12 sprigs rosemary for garnish if using, and mince enough rosemary, basil, savory, and thyme to measure ¾ teaspoon each; mince enough parsley to measure 1 tablespoon.
2. Follow zucchini recipe steps 1 through 4, Roquefort sauce recipe step 1, and lamb chops recipe steps 1 through 4.
3. While garlic cooks, follow Roquefort sauce recipe steps 2 through 5.
4. Follow lamb chops recipe steps 5 and 6 and zucchini recipe step 5.
5. Follow potato cake recipe steps 1 through 3.
6. While potatoes cook, follow zucchini recipe step 6 and lamb chops recipe steps 7 and 8.
7. Follow potato cake recipe step 4 and lamb chops recipe step 9.
8. While lamb chops are cooking, follow potato cake recipe step 5.
9. Follow lamb chops recipe steps 10 through 12.
10. Follow zucchini recipe step 7, Roquefort sauce recipe step 6, and serve with lamb chops and potato cake.

RECIPES

Lamb Chops with Fresh Herbs, Garlic, and Roquefort Sauce

¾ teaspoon minced rosemary, plus 10 to 12 sprigs for garnish (optional)
¾ teaspoon each minced thyme, savory, and basil
16 cloves garlic
Four ½- to ¾-inch-thick loin lamb chops (about 1¼ pounds total weight)
Salt and freshly ground pepper
1 tablespoon good-quality olive oil
5 tablespoons unsalted butter
¼ cup dry white wine
1 tablespoon minced parsley
Roquefort Sauce (see following recipe)

1. Preheat oven to 200 degrees.
2. Combine minced rosemary, thyme, savory, and basil in small bowl; set aside.
3. Fill medium-size saucepan with water, cover, and bring to a boil over high heat.
4. Add whole, unpeeled garlic cloves to boiling water and boil about 10 minutes, or until softened.
5. Turn garlic into strainer; set aside to cool.
6. Pat lamb chops dry with paper towels and season with salt and pepper. Sprinkle chops with herbs and press lightly to make them adhere.
7. In medium-size heavy-gauge nonaluminum skillet, heat

olive oil and 2 tablespoons butter over medium heat. When foam subsides, add chops and cook 3 minutes.

8. Meanwhile, peel garlic by gently pressing cloves out of their skins.

9. Using tongs, turn chops; add garlic and toss to coat with fat. Cook chops and garlic over medium heat, covered, 3 to 5 more minutes for rare meat, 5 to 7 minutes for medium, or 7 to 8 minutes for well done.

10. Transfer chops only to heatproof serving platter and keep warm in oven.

11. Increase heat under skillet to high and sauté garlic 1 more minute, or until golden. Pour off fat from skillet. Add wine and boil 2 to 3 minutes, or until reduced to 2 tablespoons. Still over high heat, add remaining 3 tablespoons butter, a little at a time, stirring, until butter is incorporated.

12. Remove chops from oven. Drain any accumulated juices from platter into skillet and stir until incorporated. Spoon pan liquid and garlic cloves over chops, sprinkle with parsley, and surround chops with rosemary sprigs, if desired. Serve with Roquefort sauce on the side.

Roquefort Sauce

¼ cup walnut pieces
2 ounces Roquefort cheese
3 tablespoons unsalted butter
1 shallot
½ cup dry white wine
1 cup heavy cream, approximately
Cayenne pepper

1. In small bowl, combine walnuts and Roquefort. Cut butter into small pieces; set aside. Peel and mince shallot.

2. Combine shallot and wine in small heavy-gauge non-aluminum saucepan and boil over medium-high heat 3 minutes, or until liquid is reduced to ¼ cup. Add cream and boil 3 to 4 minutes, or until sauce is reduced to ¾ cup.

3. Transfer mixture to food processor or blender and process until smooth.

4. With motor running, add Roquefort mixture, a little at a time, and butter, piece by piece, and process until smooth. Season with Cayenne pepper to taste.

5. Return sauce to small saucepan and keep warm off heat in larger pan filled with hot (but not boiling) tap water. Sauce will thin as it sits.

6. Transfer sauce to small pitcher or sauceboat. If it is still too thick to pour, add a little more cream.

Zucchini Noodles with Pistou Sauce

2 cloves garlic
1 lemon
2 ounces Parmesan cheese, preferably imported
2 plum tomatoes (about ½ pound total weight)
7-ounce jar Niçoise or other small imported black olives
4 small zucchini (about 1½ pounds total weight)
2 teaspoons salt, approximately
1 cup packed basil leaves

½ cup good-quality olive oil
Freshly ground pepper
2 tablespoons unsalted butter

1. Crush garlic under flat blade of chef's knife; remove and discard peels. Coarsely chop garlic. Halve lemon.

2. In food processor fitted with steel blade, or with grater, grate enough Parmesan to measure ½ cup. Transfer Parmesan to small bowl and set aside.

3. Wash and dry tomatoes. Cut into large dice and set aside. Drain olives and set aside.

4. Wash and dry zucchini; trim but do not peel. Cut zucchini *lengthwise* into ¼-inch-thick slices. Stack slices and cut lengthwise into thin strands. Transfer zucchini to colander, sprinkle with 2 teaspoons salt, and toss until evenly coated. Set aside to drain 20 minutes.

5. In food processor or blender, combine garlic, Parmesan, basil, and ¼ cup olive oil and purée. With motor running, add remaining oil in a slow, steady stream and process until mixture is smooth and pastelike. Squeeze in lemon juice, a drop at a time, to taste. Add salt and pepper to taste, and transfer sauce to large serving bowl.

6. Squeeze zucchini dry in paper towels. In large skillet, melt butter over medium-high heat. When foam subsides, add zucchini and sauté 3 to 5 minutes, or just until tender. Remove skillet from heat and set zucchini aside to cool.

7. When ready to serve, transfer zucchini to bowl with sauce and toss to coat. Taste and adjust seasonings. Top zucchini with tomatoes and olives and serve.

Potato Cake

1½ pounds all-purpose potatoes
⅛ teaspoon nutmeg
1 teaspoon salt
Freshly ground pepper
3 tablespoons unsalted butter
2 tablespoons good-quality olive oil

1. Fill medium-size bowl two-thirds full with cold water. Peel potatoes, dropping each potato into water as you finish peeling it. One by one, pat potatoes dry with paper towels and grate in food processor fitted with shredding disk, or on coarse side of grater. You should have about 4 cups shredded potatoes. Squeeze potatoes dry in kitchen towel, return to dried medium-size bowl, and add nutmeg, salt, and pepper to taste.

2. In 10-inch nonstick skillet, heat 1½ tablespoons butter and 1 tablespoon olive oil over medium-high heat.

3. When foam subsides, add potatoes, pressing them down with back of spoon to make an even layer, and cook 2 minutes. Reduce heat to medium-low and cook 10 more minutes, or until underside of cake is golden brown.

4. Using 2 large metal spatulas, invert cake onto large plate. Add remaining butter and olive oil to skillet and slide cake back into skillet. Cook cake over medium-low heat 5 to 7 minutes, or until tender.

5. Slide cake onto heatproof serving platter and keep warm in 200-degree oven until ready to serve.

Jean Anderson

MENU 1 (Right)
Minted Buttermilk and Radish Soup
Lemon-Marinated Swordfish Kabobs
Carrot and Coriander Pilaf Salad

MENU 2
Falafel Cutlets with Tahini Sauce
Cucumbers with Mint and Yogurt
Red Onion and Orange Salad with Fresh Basil

MENU 3
Sautéed Chicken Breasts with
Walnut-Yogurt Sauce
Tabbouleh Salad
Melon Kabobs with Honey and
Orange-Flower Water

After many trips through the Middle East, Jean Anderson has developed her own repertoire of Middle Eastern dishes. Although she alters and adapts traditional recipes to suit American ingredients, she manages to preserve authentic tastes. In Menu 1, she re-creates a refreshing cold soup, based on buttermilk and chopped radishes, that she once tasted in Beirut. The entrée—broiled lemon-marinated swordfish kabobs and an aromatic rice salad with carrots and coriander—is also Lebanese.

Inhabitants of the eastern Mediterranean love *falafel* in pita bread as much as Americans love hamburgers on buns. A popular fast food sold at sidewalk stands, *falafel* (traditionally made of ground chickpeas shaped into balls and deep fried) is the featured dish of Menu 2. Here, the cook shapes the *falafel* into cutlets, which she browns quickly, then tops with a nutty sauce made with *tahini* (sesame seed paste). Cucumber crescents with mint and yogurt and a light salad of red onions and oranges are the refreshing accompaniments.

Menu 3 presents a streamlined version of a Middle Eastern classic—chicken in walnut-yogurt sauce—that would normally take well over an hour to prepare. This recipe calls for boned and flattened chicken breasts, which are sautéed in a matter of minutes. With the chicken, Jean Anderson serves *tabbouleh* salad and, at the meal's end, jewel-like pieces of macerated melon threaded on skewers, a variation on a dessert she once enjoyed in Cairo.

To create a truly Middle Eastern atmosphere for this meal, serve the buttermilk and radish soup, swordfish kabobs, and rice pilaf salad on a colorful carpet.

74

Minted Buttermilk and Radish Soup
Lemon-Marinated Swordfish Kabobs
Carrot and Coriander Pilaf Salad

If fresh swordfish is unavailable, the cook suggests substituting fresh salmon steaks rather than frozen swordfish; frozen fish tends to exude so much liquid that it dilutes the marinade.

WHAT TO DRINK

To complement this menu, try a very crisp, dry white wine, such as a French Sancerre or Muscadet.

SHOPPING LIST AND STAPLES

Four 1¼-inch-thick swordfish steaks (about 1½ pounds total weight)
Large bunch radishes
Small head romaine lettuce
2 medium-size carrots
1 medium-size plus 1 small yellow onion
1 large plus 1 small clove garlic
Small bunch fresh coriander, if available
Small bunch flat-leaf parsley, if not using coriander
Small bunch fresh mint, or 4 teaspoons dried
15 large bay leaves, preferably fresh, or dried
3 large lemons
1 quart buttermilk
5 cups chicken stock, preferably homemade (see page 9), or canned
5 tablespoons good-quality olive oil
1 cup converted white rice
1 teaspoon dried basil
½ teaspoon dried thyme
¼ teaspoon ground coriander, plus ¼ teaspoon if not using fresh
⅛ teaspoon ground cumin
Salt and freshly ground pepper

UTENSILS

Food processor or blender
Large heavy-gauge saucepan with cover
Medium-size heavy-gauge saucepan
Large glass or ceramic dish
13 x 9 x 2-inch flameproof baking pan
2 large bowls
2 small bowls
Large strainer
Measuring cups and spoons

Chef's knife
Paring knife
2 wooden spoons
Four 15-inch metal skewers
Vegetable peeler

START-TO-FINISH STEPS

1. Peel onions. Quarter small onion for soup recipe. Coarsely chop enough of large onion to measure 1 cup for salad recipe; set aside. Crush and peel garlic. Set aside large clove for soup recipe and mince enough of small clove to measure 1 teaspoon for salad recipe; set aside. Wash and dry coriander or parsley, and fresh mint and bay leaves if using, and dry with paper towels. Mince enough coriander or parsley to measure ⅓ cup for salad recipe. Set aside 4 mint sprigs for garnish, if using, and mince enough remaining mint to measure ⅓ cup for soup recipe. Set aside.
2. Follow soup recipe steps 1 and 2 and swordfish recipe steps 1 through 3.
3. While swordfish marinates, follow soup recipe steps 3 and 4 and salad recipe steps 1 through 4.
4. Fifteen minutes before serving time, follow swordfish recipe steps 4 and 5.
5. While swordfish kabobs are broiling, follow soup recipe step 5 and salad recipe step 5.
6. Follow swordfish recipe step 6 and serve with soup and salad.

RECIPES

Minted Buttermilk and Radish Soup

3 cups chicken stock
Small yellow onion, quartered
Large clove garlic, crushed and peeled
1 teaspoon dried basil
¼ teaspoon dried thyme
¼ teaspoon salt
⅛ teaspoon freshly ground pepper
Large bunch radishes
1½ cups buttermilk
⅓ cup chopped fresh mint, or 4 teaspoons dried
4 mint sprigs for garnish (optional)

1. Heat stock in large heavy-gauge saucepan over medium heat until hot. Add onion, garlic, basil, thyme, salt, and pepper, and simmer, covered, 15 minutes.

2. Meanwhile, wash and dry radishes. Trim radishes and reserve 4 for garnish, if desired. Coarsely chop remaining radishes; you should have about 1⅓ cups. Place chopped radishes in small bowl; cover with plastic wrap. If using radishes for garnish, cut decoratively and immerse in small bowl of ice water; cover bowls and refrigerate until ready to serve.

3. Turn stock into large strainer set over large bowl. Transfer solids remaining in strainer to food processor or blender. Add 1 cup stock and process 15 seconds, or until mixture is puréed. Return purée to bowl with stock.

4. Stir in buttermilk and dried mint, if using. (Do not add fresh mint at this point.) Cover bowl with plastic wrap and place in freezer to chill until serving time.

5. To serve, divide soup among 4 bowls. Sprinkle each serving with chopped radishes, and chopped fresh mint if using, and garnish with a whole radish and a mint sprig, if desired.

Lemon-Marinated Swordfish Kabobs

3 large lemons
3 tablespoons good-quality olive oil
15 large bay leaves, preferably fresh, or dried
¼ teaspoon freshly ground pepper
Four 1¼-inch-thick swordfish steaks (about 1½ pounds total weight)

1. Wash and dry lemons. Using vegetable peeler, remove zest from 1 lemon in long, thin strips, avoiding white pith as much as possible. Halve peeled lemon and squeeze enough juice to measure ¼ cup. Cut remaining lemons into 12 wedges.

2. For marinade, combine lemon zest, lemon juice, olive oil, 3 bay leaves, and pepper in glass or ceramic dish large enough to hold swordfish steaks in one layer.

3. Rinse swordfish and dry with paper towels. Cut swordfish into approximately sixteen 1½-inch cubes. Add swordfish to marinade and toss to coat well. Cover dish with plastic wrap and refrigerate at least 30 minutes.

4. Preheat broiler. Thread swordfish cubes alternately with lemon wedges and remaining bay leaves on four 15-inch metal skewers. Balance skewers lengthwise on 13 x 9 x 2-inch flameproof baking pan. Drizzle kabobs with marinade.

5. Broil kabobs 4 inches from heat 5 minutes. Turn skewers over and broil another 5 minutes.

6. Divide kabobs among 4 dinner plates and serve.

Carrot and Coriander Pilaf Salad

2 medium-size carrots
Small head romaine lettuce
2 tablespoons good-quality olive oil
1 teaspoon minced garlic
1 cup coarsely chopped onion
¼ teaspoon ground coriander, plus ¼ teaspoon if not using fresh
¼ teaspoon dried thyme
⅛ teaspoon ground cumin
⅛ teaspoon freshly ground pepper

1 cup converted white rice
2 cups chicken stock
½ teaspoon salt
⅓ cup chopped fresh coriander or flat-leaf parsley

1. Wash and dry carrots. Coarsely chop carrots. Wash and dry 4 large romaine leaves. Place leaves in plastic bag and refrigerate until ready to use. Reserve remaining romaine for another use.

2. Heat oil over medium-high heat in medium-size heavy-gauge saucepan 1 minute. Add carrots, garlic, and onion, and sauté, stirring, 2 to 3 minutes, or until onion is golden.

3. Add ground coriander, thyme, cumin, pepper, and rice, and stir 30 seconds. Reduce heat to medium-low, add stock and salt, and simmer, uncovered, 18 to 20 minutes, or until rice is tender and all liquid is absorbed.

4. Transfer rice to large bowl. Add fresh coriander or parsley and toss lightly to combine. Cover salad loosely and let stand at room temperature until ready to serve.

5. To serve, place 1 romaine leaf on each of 4 dinner plates and divide salad among leaves.

ADDED TOUCH

Adjust the amount of sugar to your taste in this tart and refreshing ruby-red dessert.

Cranberry-Tangerine Sorbet

¾ pound fresh cranberries, or 12-ounce bag frozen cranberries, partially thawed
3 medium-size tangerines (about 1 pound total weight)
⅓ cup sugar
1 cup light corn syrup

1. Place cranberries in colander and rinse. Remove and discard any stems or imperfect berries. Set cranberries aside to drain.

2. Wash and dry tangerines. Remove 4 long strips of rind from 1 tangerine, avoiding white pith as much as possible; set aside. Halve tangerines and squeeze enough juice to measure 1 cup.

3. Transfer cranberries to food processor fitted with steel blade; pulse 10 to 12 times to chop coarsely. Or, chop cranberries with chef's knife.

4. Combine cranberries and 2 cups water in medium-size heavy-gauge saucepan. Bring liquid to a boil over high heat, reduce heat to medium, and simmer berries 5 minutes.

5. Turn cranberries into fine sieve set over large bowl. Using wooden spoon or spatula, force as much cranberry pulp as possible through sieve.

6. Add tangerine juice, sugar, and corn syrup to bowl and stir until sugar dissolves.

7. Pour mixture into 9-inch square glass baking dish and freeze at least 3 hours, or until firm.

8. Remove sorbet from freezer 20 to 30 minutes before serving and let stand at room temperature to soften.

9. Spoon sorbet into stemmed goblets or dessert dishes and garnish each serving with a strip of tangerine rind.

Falafel Cutlets with Tahini Sauce
Cucumbers with Mint and Yogurt
Red Onion and Orange Salad with Fresh Basil

Filling falafel *cutlets, fragrant with Eastern spices, need only light salads and pita bread as accompaniments.*

Chickpeas are the foundation of *falafel.* Although the cook prefers dried chickpeas for most Middle Eastern recipes, she uses the canned variety for this one because they are soft and bind well with the other ingredients. For frying the *falafel* cutlets, use a mixture of dark sesame oil and peanut oil. If sesame oil is unavailable or seems too costly, use peanut oil only.

Tahini, a thick paste made of ground raw white sesame seeds, is a popular Middle Eastern condiment. It is readily available in most well-stocked supermarkets and in Middle Eastern markets and health food stores. Because *tahini* turns rancid quickly, refrigerate it after opening and use it within a month. When stored, the oil tends to separate from the paste, so stir the *tahini* to blend it before each use.

WHAT TO DRINK

Ice-cold beer or ale is the best beverage here, though you might prefer to serve a well-chilled Alsace Gewürztraminer or Riesling instead.

SHOPPING LIST AND STAPLES

3 medium-size cucumbers (about 2 pounds total weight)
Small head romaine lettuce
2 small red onions (about ½ pound total weight)
Small yellow onion
2 large cloves plus 1 small clove garlic
Small bunch parsley
Small bunch mint
Small bunch basil
3 large navel oranges
3 medium-size lemons
Large egg
¼ cup milk
1 pint sour cream
8-ounce container plain low-fat yogurt
20-ounce can chickpeas
4-ounce jar tahini
4-ounce bottle dark sesame oil
¼ cup good-quality olive oil
2 tablespoons peanut oil, approximately

2 tablespoons honey
5 slices firm-textured white bread
¾ cup fine dried bread crumbs
¾ teaspoon dried thyme
½ teaspoon dried marjoram
1¼ teaspoons paprika
¾ teaspoon ground cumin, approximately
½ teaspoon Cayenne pepper
½ teaspoon ground coriander
Salt and freshly ground black pepper

UTENSILS

Food processor or blender
Large heavy-gauge skillet
Large baking sheet
2 large bowls, 1 nonaluminum
2 medium-size bowls
Small bowl
Colander
Measuring cups and spoons
Chef's knife
Paring knife
Metal spatula
Vegetable peeler

START-TO-FINISH STEPS

1. Crush and peel 1 large and 1 small clove garlic for falafel and cucumbers recipes. Peel and quarter 1 large clove garlic for salad recipe; set aside. Halve 1 lemon and cut into 8 thin slices for falafel recipe. Halve remaining lemons and squeeze enough juice to measure 3 tablespoons for salad recipe and 4 teaspoons for tahini sauce recipe. Peel onions. Quarter yellow onion for falafel recipe and cut enough red onions into ½-inch-thick slices to measure 1½ cups for salad recipe. Wash and dry fresh herbs. Set aside 4 parsley sprigs for garnish and measure ⅓ cup loosely packed sprigs for falafel recipe. Set aside 12 mint sprigs for garnish and finely chop enough mint to measure ⅓ cup for cucumbers recipe. Coarsely chop enough basil leaves to measure ⅓ cup for salad recipe.
2. Follow falafel recipe steps 1 through 4 and rinse food processor or blender.
3. While falafel chills, follow salad recipe steps 1 and 2 and cucumbers recipe steps 1 and 2.
4. Follow tahini sauce recipe steps 1 and 2.
5. Follow salad recipe step 3 and falafel recipe steps 5 and 6.
6. Follow cucumbers recipe step 3 and salad recipe step 4.
7. Follow falafel recipe step 7 and serve with cucumbers and salad.

RECIPES

Falafel Cutlets with Tahini Sauce

20-ounce can chickpeas
5 slices firm-textured white bread

⅓ cup loosely packed parsley sprigs, plus 4 sprigs
    for garnish
½ teaspoon dried marjoram
¾ teaspoon salt
1¼ teaspoons paprika
¼ teaspoon dried thyme
¼ teaspoon ground coriander
¼ teaspoon Cayenne pepper
⅛ teaspoon ground cumin
⅛ teaspoon freshly ground black pepper
Small yellow onion, quartered
Large clove garlic, crushed and peeled
Large egg
1 tablespoon tahini
¾ cup fine dried bread crumbs
1 tablespoon dark sesame oil
2 tablespoons peanut oil, approximately
Tahini Sauce (see following recipe)
8 lemon slices for garnish

1. Rinse and drain chickpeas in colander and pat dry with paper towels.
2. Tear or cut bread into small pieces. In food processor fitted with steel blade, or in blender, combine bread, ⅓ cup parsley, marjoram, salt, ½ teaspoon paprika, thyme, coriander, Cayenne pepper, cumin, and black pepper. Process until bread is reduced to crumbs. Transfer mixture to large bowl.
3. In food processor or blender, combine chickpeas, onion, and garlic, and process until finely chopped. Add to bread-crumb mixture, and stir to combine. Add egg and tahini and stir until well blended.
4. Spoon falafel mixture onto large sheet of aluminum foil, flatten to 1 inch thick, and freeze, wrapped in foil, 20 minutes.
5. Spread dried bread crumbs on plate. Line large baking sheet with waxed paper. Divide falafel mixture into 4 equal portions. Flatten each portion into 6-inch oval cutlet about ¾ inch thick, and dredge each cutlet in dried bread crumbs, pressing to help them adhere. Using metal spatula, transfer cutlets to baking sheet.
6. Heat sesame oil and peanut oil in large heavy-gauge skillet over high heat 1 minute, or until almost smoking. Using spatula, carefully add cutlets and brown 3 minutes on one side. Turn cutlets and brown another 2 minutes, adding more peanut oil if necessary.
7. Divide cutlets among 4 dinner plates. Top with some tahini sauce and sprinkle with remaining paprika. Garnish with lemon slices and parsley sprigs. Serve remaining sauce separately.

Tahini Sauce

1¼ cups sour cream
⅓ cup tahini
¼ cup milk
4 teaspoons freshly squeezed lemon juice
½ teaspoon salt
¼ teaspoon ground coriander

¼ teaspoon ground cumin
¼ teaspoon dried thyme
¼ teaspoon Cayenne pepper

1. Combine all ingredients in container of food processor or blender and process until smooth.
2. Transfer sauce to medium-size bowl, cover with plastic wrap, and set aside at room temperature until ready to serve.

Cucumbers with Mint and Yogurt

3 medium-size cucumbers (about 2 pounds total weight)
1 cup plain low-fat yogurt
⅓ cup finely chopped mint, plus 12 sprigs for garnish
¼ teaspoon ground cumin
Small clove garlic, crushed and peeled
¼ teaspoon salt
⅛ teaspoon freshly ground pepper

1. Peel and trim cucumbers and halve lengthwise. Scoop out seeds with spoon and invert halves onto paper towels to drain.
2. Combine yogurt, chopped mint, cumin, garlic, salt, and pepper in medium-size bowl, and stir to blend. Cover with plastic wrap and set aside.
3. Just before serving, remove garlic clove from yogurt, if desired. Cut cucumber halves crosswise into ½-inch slices. Add slices to yogurt mixture and toss lightly. Divide cucumbers among 4 dinner plates and garnish each serving with 3 mint sprigs.

Red Onion and Orange Salad with Fresh Basil

Small head romaine lettuce
3 large navel oranges
¼ cup good-quality olive oil
3 tablespoons freshly squeezed lemon juice
2 tablespoons honey
⅓ cup coarsely chopped fresh basil
¼ teaspoon dried thyme
⅛ teaspoon freshly ground pepper
Large clove garlic, peeled and quartered
1½ cups sliced red onions

1. Wash romaine and remove any bruised or discolored leaves. Remove 8 leaves and pat dry with paper towels. Wrap leaves in plastic bag and refrigerate until ready to use. Reserve remaining lettuce for another use. Peel oranges, removing all of white pith, and cut crosswise into ¼-inch-thick slices.
2. Combine oil, lemon juice, honey, basil, thyme, pepper, and garlic in small bowl, and stir to blend. Set aside at least 10 minutes to allow flavors to meld.
3. Place one third of orange slices in large nonaluminum bowl and top with one third of onion slices. Discard garlic from dressing and drizzle one third of dressing over salad. Layer remaining oranges, onion, and dressing in same manner. Set aside until ready to serve.
4. To serve, divide lettuce among 4 dinner plates and top with salad.

ADDED TOUCH

This bright-yellow pudding, which is studded with pistachios and candied fruits, is well worth the lengthy preparation time. For the best flavor, make the pudding a day or two ahead, refrigerate it, and unmold it just before serving.

Saffron Rice Pudding with Wildflower Honey Sauce

2½ cups milk
¼ teaspoon saffron threads
½ cup long-grain white rice
¼ cup chopped mixed candied fruits
¼ cup chopped blanched pistachio nuts
1 envelope unflavored gelatin (1 tablespoon)
⅔ cup granulated sugar
4 egg yolks
½ teaspoon vanilla extract
¼ teaspoon almond extract
1 cup plain low-fat yogurt

Wildflower Honey Sauce:
⅓ cup wildflower honey
1 tablespoon freshly squeezed lemon juice
Pinch of cinnamon

1. Pour 1½ cups milk into small heavy-gauge saucepan. Crush saffron threads and add to milk. Bring mixture to a boil over medium heat. When milk boils, reduce heat to low and stir in rice. Cook rice, uncovered, 10 minutes. Cover pan and cook another 10 to 15 minutes, or until rice is tender and all milk is absorbed.
2. Transfer rice to large bowl and stir in candied fruits and 3 tablespoons pistachios.
3. In same small saucepan, combine remaining 1 cup milk, gelatin, and sugar. Cook mixture over low heat, stirring constantly, 5 minutes, or until gelatin dissolves completely. Remove from heat and set aside.
4. In small bowl, beat egg yolks lightly. Whisk a little hot-milk mixture into yolks, pour yolk mixture back into pan, and whisk until combined. Cook over low heat, stirring, 3 to 5 minutes, or until mixture becomes slightly thickened.
5. Remove pan from heat and stir milk mixture into rice. Add vanilla, almond extract, and yogurt, and stir to combine. Set pudding aside to cool 30 minutes. Meanwhile, butter 2-quart melon-shaped mold or other decorative 2-quart mold.
6. When cooled, stir pudding well and spoon into prepared mold. Cover mold with plastic wrap and chill 3 to 4 hours, or until pudding is firm.
7. Meanwhile, prepare wildflower honey sauce: Combine honey, lemon juice, and cinnamon in small bowl. Stir to combine and set aside.
8. To unmold pudding, dip mold briefly in hot water and invert over small serving platter. Top pudding with some sauce and sprinkle with remaining 1 tablespoon pistachios. Serve remaining sauce separately.

Sautéed Chicken Breasts with Walnut-Yogurt Sauce
Tabbouleh Salad
Melon Kabobs with Honey and Orange-Flower Water

Let everyone help themselves to chicken with walnut-yogurt sauce, tabbouleh *salad, and skewered melon pieces.*

Every Middle Eastern country has its own version of *tabbouleh*, a cracked-wheat salad with chopped tomato, parsley, mint, and olive oil. This Jordanian recipe calls for bulgur, a type of wheat that has been steamed and dried. Because of the processing, bulgur needs only brief soaking in boiling water to be ready for the salad.

WHAT TO DRINK

An acidic or full-bodied white wine would make a good foil for these dishes. If you like acidic liveliness, choose an Italian Pinot Grigio or Verdicchio; for fuller body, select a California Chardonnay or Pinot Blanc.

SHOPPING LIST AND STAPLES

2 whole skinless, boneless chicken breasts, pounded thin (about 1¼ pounds total weight)
5 medium-size plum tomatoes (about 1 pound total weight)
Medium-size carrot
1 small plus 2 medium-size yellow onions
Medium-size clove garlic
Large bunch parsley
Small bunch mint
Small cantaloupe (about 2 pounds)
Small honeydew melon (about 2½ pounds)
2 lemons
8-ounce container plain low-fat yogurt
1 cup chicken stock, preferably homemade (see page 9), or canned
⅓ cup good-quality olive oil, approximately
⅓ cup honey
4-ounce bottle orange-flower water
8-ounce package bulgur
3-ounce can walnut pieces
1 slice firm-textured white bread
2 teaspoons sweet paprika
½ teaspoon dried marjoram
¼ teaspoon dried thyme
Salt and freshly ground pepper

UTENSILS

Food processor or blender
Large heavy-gauge skillet
2 small saucepans, 1 heavy-gauge

2 large nonaluminum bowls
Large heatproof bowl
Medium-size nonaluminum bowl
3 small bowls
Large fine sieve
Measuring cups and spoons
Chef's knife
Paring knife
2 wooden spoons
Rubber spatula
Citrus juicer (optional)
Ladle
Whisk
Metal tongs
Four 12-inch skewers
Melon baller

START-TO-FINISH STEPS

1. Peel onions. Quarter small onion for chicken recipe. Coarsely chop medium-size onions for salad recipe; set aside. Halve lemons and squeeze enough juice to measure 2 tablespoons for salad recipe, 2 tablespoons for melon recipe, and 1½ teaspoons for chicken recipe. Wash and dry parsley and mint. Coarsely chop enough parsley to measure ⅓ cup for salad recipe and finely chop enough to measure 1 teaspoon for chicken recipe. Reserve 10 mint sprigs for melon recipe and coarsely chop enough mint to measure ¼ cup for salad recipe.

2. Follow chicken recipe steps 1 through 3.

3. While stock simmers, follow salad recipe steps 1 through 4 and melon recipe steps 1 and 2.

4. Follow chicken recipe steps 4 and 5 and salad recipe step 5.

5. Follow chicken recipe steps 6 and 7.

6. Follow salad recipe step 6, chicken recipe step 8, and serve.

7. Follow melon recipe step 3 and serve for dessert.

RECIPES

Sautéed Chicken Breasts with Walnut-Yogurt Sauce

Medium-size clove garlic
Medium-size carrot
1 cup chicken stock
Small yellow onion, quartered

½ teaspoon dried marjoram
¼ teaspoon dried thyme
1 slice firm-textured white bread
¾ cup walnut pieces
2 teaspoons sweet paprika
1½ teaspoons freshly squeezed lemon juice
¼ teaspoon salt
⅛ teaspoon freshly ground pepper
½ cup plain low-fat yogurt
2 whole skinless, boneless chicken breasts, pounded
    thin (about 1¼ pounds total weight)
4 teaspoons good-quality olive oil
1 teaspoon finely chopped parsley for garnish

1. Crush and peel garlic. Peel, trim, and thinly slice carrot into rounds.
2. Combine stock, garlic, carrot, onion, marjoram, and thyme in small heavy-gauge saucepan. Bring mixture to a boil over high heat, reduce heat to medium-low, and simmer 25 minutes.
3. Meanwhile, tear bread into small pieces and place in food processor or blender with ½ cup walnuts and paprika. Process until bread is reduced to fine crumbs; transfer to small bowl and set aside.
4. After stock mixture has cooked, remove ½ cup liquid from saucepan and set aside in another small bowl.
5. Transfer remaining stock mixture to food processor or blender. Add bread-crumb mixture, lemon juice, salt, pepper, and yogurt, and process until well combined. Transfer walnut-yogurt sauce to medium-size nonaluminum bowl, cover loosely with plastic wrap, and set aside.
6. Rinse chicken breasts and dry with paper towels. Heat oil in large heavy-gauge skillet over high heat 1 to 1½ minutes, or until almost smoking. Add chicken breasts, reduce heat to medium-high, and sauté chicken 3 to 4 minutes on one side, or until browned. Using tongs, turn chicken and sauté another 3 to 4 minutes. Transfer chicken to serving platter and keep warm on stove top.
7. Add reserved ½ cup stock to skillet and boil over high heat 1 minute, scraping up browned bits from bottom of pan. Pour into walnut-yogurt sauce and stir to combine.
8. To serve, spoon sauce over chicken and sprinkle with remaining ¼ cup walnut pieces and finely chopped parsley.

Tabbouleh Salad

5 medium-size plum tomatoes
    (about 1 pound total weight)

¾ cup bulgur
⅓ cup coarsely chopped parsley
¼ cup coarsely chopped mint
2 medium-size yellow onions, coarsely chopped
¼ cup good-quality olive oil
2 tablespoons freshly squeezed lemon juice
1½ teaspoons salt
⅛ teaspoon freshly ground pepper

1. Bring 1½ cups water to a boil in small saucepan over high heat.
2. Meanwhile, wash tomatoes and dry with paper towels. Coarsely chop 4 tomatoes; cut remaining tomato lengthwise into wedges. Set aside.
3. Place bulgur in large heatproof bowl. Add boiling water, stir, and let mixture stand 20 minutes.
4. Meanwhile, combine chopped tomatoes, parsley, mint, onions, olive oil, lemon juice, salt, and pepper in large nonaluminum bowl.
5. After 20 minutes, turn bulgur into large fine sieve and drain very well. Add bulgur to tomato mixture and toss to combine; set aside until ready to serve.
6. To serve, toss salad again and mound on serving platter. Garnish with tomato wedges.

Melon Kabobs with Honey and Orange-Flower Water

Small cantaloupe (about 2 pounds)
Small honeydew melon (about 2½ pounds)
⅓ cup honey
2 tablespoons freshly squeezed lemon juice
1 tablespoon orange-flower water
10 mint sprigs for garnish

1. Halve melons and discard seeds. Cut cantaloupe lengthwise into 1½-inch-wide wedges; trim off and discard rind. Cut cantaloupe wedges into 1½-inch cubes and place in large nonaluminum bowl. Using large end of melon baller, scoop flesh of honeydew melon into balls; add to bowl with cantaloupe.
2. Place honey, lemon juice, and orange-flower water in small bowl and whisk to combine. Pour over melon and toss well. Cover bowl and refrigerate until shortly before serving.
3. To serve, skewer cantaloupe cubes and honeydew balls alternately on four 12-inch skewers. Place skewers on serving dish and garnish with mint.

Joyce Goldstein

MENU 1 (Left)
Portuguese Chicken Soup
Steamed Clams and Sausage in Spicy Sauce
Mixed Green Salad

MENU 2
Spinach Soup with Yogurt
Turkish Broiled Chicken
Pilaf with Currants and Pistachios

MENU 3
Garlic and Bread Soup
Pork with Peppers and Onions
Portuguese-style Fried Potatoes

An ardent world traveler, Joyce Goldstein attributes her eclectic cooking style to her fascination with international cuisines, particularly the foods of the Mediterranean. Unlike many of her contemporaries, who prefer to experiment with recipes, she sticks to tradition. "I am a classicist and a scholar," she says. "I research dishes in numerous cookbooks, and from seven versions of the same recipe I will pick the one that seems truest and then follow it exactly." As a consequence, when you sample her dinners—two from Portugal and one from Turkey—you will have eaten as the natives do.

The dramatic Portuguese main dish of clams and sausage (*amêijoas na cataplana*) in Menu 1 is from the Algarve region. Traditionally it is cooked in a *cataplana*, a clam-shaped copper cooking vessel with a tight-fitting lid, which you open at the table for an appetizing burst of aromas. However, as Joyce Goldstein shows, you can prepare this dish just as successfully in a covered sauté pan.

Menu 3, also from Portugal, begins with a lusty garlic and bread soup, followed by sweet-tart pork with peppers and onions from the Alenteja region. The fried new potatoes—a ubiquitous Portuguese dish—may be served on one side of the plate or, more traditionally, arranged in a ring around the meat.

For the Turkish dinner of Menu 2, the cook presents a spinach soup with yogurt, then offers broiled marinated chicken, and a pilaf enlivened with currants and toasted pistachios. The marinade for the chicken, a mixture of olive oil, lemon juice, onion, garlic, and cinnamon, may be used on cubed lamb as well.

This Portuguese meal begins with a rich chicken soup flavored with lemon and mint. Follow the soup with spicy clams and sausage and a light tossed salad.

Portuguese Chicken Soup
Steamed Clams and Sausage in Spicy Sauce
Mixed Green Salad

Littlenecks are hard-shelled clams native to the coastal waters off New England and Long Island. If you cannot get littlenecks, use whatever small clams are available in your local fish market. Select only those clams with tightly closed shells. After you bring the clams home, scrub them with a stiff brush under cold water, and discard any with cracked or broken shells. Once cooked, discard any that do not open.

Spicy, garlicky Portuguese *linguiça* sausage—or the similar Spanish *chorizo*—is often added to cooked dishes for a flavor accent. Look for these sausages in Latin American or Caribbean markets or in well-stocked supermarkets. Smoked and dry-cured *linguiça* keeps well at room temperature for several days; made of fresh pork, *chorizo* requires refrigeration. If you like, serve the clams and sausage with a loaf or two of crusty bread, or spooned over white rice.

WHAT TO DRINK

You could drink a white or a red wine with this meal, but in either case, your first choice should be Portuguese. Try a Dão for the red; a crisp, clean Vinho Verde for the white. If Portuguese wine is not available, serve a white or red Spanish Rioja.

SHOPPING LIST AND STAPLES

24 to 36 littleneck clams
1 whole skinless, boneless chicken breast (about 1 pound)
¾ pound linguiça or chorizo sausage
⅓ pound prosciutto (6 to 7 medium-thin slices)
Small head romaine lettuce
1 head Boston or small head red leaf lettuce
1 bunch watercress
1 small plus 2 medium-size red onions
6 medium-size cloves garlic
Small bunch parsley
Small bunch mint
Small bunch coriander (optional)
2 large lemons
35-ounce can Italian plum tomatoes
4 cups chicken stock, preferably homemade (see page 9), or canned
1 cup fruity olive oil
6-ounce can pitted black olives

1 cup long-grain white rice
2 teaspoons paprika
1 teaspoon dried oregano
1 teaspoon red pepper flakes, approximately
3 bay leaves
Salt and freshly ground black pepper
1 cup dry white wine

UTENSILS

Large sauté pan with cover
Medium-size saucepan
Small heavy-gauge saucepan with cover
Salad bowl
Medium-size nonaluminum bowl
Small nonaluminum bowl
Salad spinner (optional)
Strainer
Measuring cups and spoons
Chef's knife
Paring knife
2 wooden spoons
Slotted spoon
Ladle
Whisk
Citrus juicer (optional)

START-TO-FINISH STEPS

1. Wash parsley, mint, and coriander if using, and dry with paper towels. Trim stems and discard. Chop enough parsley to measure ½ cup for clams recipe. Chop enough mint to measure 6 tablespoons for soup recipe. If using coriander, chop enough to measure ⅓ cup for salad recipe. Reserve remaining herbs for another use. Squeeze enough lemon juice to measure ¼ cup each for soup and salad recipes; set aside.
2. Follow salad recipe steps 1 through 4.
3. Follow soup recipe step 1.
4. While rice simmers, follow clams recipe steps 1 through 5.
5. Follow soup recipe step 2 and clams recipe steps 6 through 11.
6. While onions are cooking, follow soup recipe steps 3 through 5.
7. While chicken simmers, follow clams recipe steps 12 and 13.

8. While sauce simmers, follow soup recipe steps 6 and 7 and serve as first course.
9. Follow clams recipe steps 14 and 15.
10. While clams are steaming, follow salad recipe step 5.
11. Follow clams recipe step 16 and serve with salad.

RECIPES

Portuguese Chicken Soup

4 cups chicken stock
1 cup long-grain white rice
1 whole skinless, boneless chicken breast (about
   1 pound)
¼ cup lemon juice
Salt and freshly ground black pepper
6 tablespoons chopped mint

1. Combine 1 cup stock and 1 cup water in small heavy-gauge saucepan and bring to a boil over high heat. Stir in rice, cover pan, and reduce heat to low. Simmer rice gently, undisturbed, about 20 minutes, or until all liquid is absorbed.
2. When rice is cooked, remove from heat and set aside, covered.
3. Pour remaining 3 cups chicken stock into medium-size saucepan and bring to a simmer over medium-high heat.
4. Meanwhile, rinse chicken breast under cold running water and dry with paper towel. Cut chicken into 1-inch-long by ½-inch-wide strips.
5. Add chicken to stock, reduce heat to medium, and simmer gently, uncovered, 3 minutes.
6. Stir in rice, lemon juice, and salt and pepper to taste.
7. Add mint, pour soup into large serving bowl, tureen, or 4 individual soup bowls, and serve immediately.

Steamed Clams and Sausage in Spicy Sauce

24 to 36 littleneck clams
2 medium-size red onions
6 medium-size cloves garlic
35-ounce can Italian plum tomatoes
¾ pound linguiça or chorizo sausage
½ cup fruity olive oil
⅓ pound prosciutto (6 to 7 medium-thin slices)
2 teaspoons paprika
1 teaspoon red pepper flakes, approximately
1 cup dry white wine
3 bay leaves
1 teaspoon dried oregano
Salt and freshly ground black pepper
½ cup chopped parsley

1. Wash clams well. Keep cold until ready to steam.
2. Peel onions and cut enough crosswise into ⅛-inch-thick slices to measure about 2 cups; set aside.
3. Crush and peel garlic and mince enough to measure 2 tablespoons; set aside.
4. Turn tomatoes into strainer set over medium-size non-aluminum bowl to drain. Reserve juice, and chop enough tomatoes to measure about 2 cups; set aside.
5. Remove casings from linguiça or chorizo and crumble meat; set aside. You should have about 2½ cups.
6. For sauce, heat 3 tablespoons olive oil in large sauté pan over medium-high heat.
7. While oil is heating, line plate with double thickness of paper towels; set aside.
8. Add sausage to pan and fry, stirring occasionally, about 3 minutes, or until fat is released.
9. Meanwhile, stack prosciutto slices and cut into 1-inch-long julienne strips; set aside.
10. Using slotted spoon, transfer sausage to paper-towel-lined plate to drain; set aside. Drain fat from pan.
11. Add remaining 5 tablespoons oil to pan and heat over medium heat until hot. Add onions and sauté, stirring occasionally, 5 minutes.
12. Add garlic, paprika, and red pepper flakes to taste to pan and stir to combine. Cook another minute.
13. Stir in sausage, prosciutto, tomatoes and their juice, wine, bay leaves, and oregano. Increase heat to medium-high and bring liquid to a boil. Lower heat to medium and simmer, uncovered, about 20 minutes.
14. Taste and adjust seasoning, adding salt and pepper to taste, and additional red pepper flakes if desired.
15. Place clams on top of simmering sauce, cover pan, and steam clams 3 to 6 minutes, or until they open.
16. Remove and discard any unopened clams. Gently turn mixture into serving dish, sprinkle with chopped parsley, and serve.

Mixed Green Salad

Small head romaine lettuce
1 head Boston or small head red leaf lettuce
1 bunch watercress
Small red onion
12 pitted black olives
½ cup fruity olive oil
¼ cup lemon juice
Salt
Freshly ground black pepper
⅓ cup chopped coriander (optional)

1. Wash greens and dry in salad spinner or with paper towels. Remove and discard any bruised or discolored leaves. Trim stems from watercress and discard. Tear greens into bite-size pieces and place in salad bowl; set aside.
2. Peel onion and cut crosswise into ⅛-inch-thick slices; add to bowl with greens.
3. Drain olives and add to salad. Cover bowl with plastic wrap and refrigerate until ready to serve.
4. For dressing, combine oil, lemon juice, and salt and pepper to taste in small nonaluminum bowl and whisk until blended; set aside.
5. Just before serving, whisk dressing to recombine and pour over salad. Toss salad until evenly coated and sprinkle with coriander, if desired.

Spinach Soup with Yogurt
Turkish Broiled Chicken
Pilaf with Currants and Pistachios

T he marinated chicken can be grilled over a charcoal or wood fire, if you prefer cooking outdoors. Place the grill about 4 inches above the coals and cook the chicken quarters skin-side up for the first 10 minutes so the underside cooks through and there is less likelihood of fire flare-up from dripping fat. During the final 10 minutes of grilling, baste the chicken with the marinade. The chicken is done when the juices run clear when it is pierced with the tip of a knife. You may want to prepare the marinade in the morning (or the night before) and let the chicken marinate, covered, in the refrigerator as long as possible.

For a festive Middle Eastern meal, first offer spinach soup with yogurt, then broiled marinated chicken and a delectable rice pilaf studded with currants and pistachios.

WHAT TO DRINK

A medium-bodied white wine, especially one with an assertive flavor, goes well with this menu. A California or Alsace Gewürztraminer would be ideal.

SHOPPING LIST AND STAPLES

2½-pound broiling chicken, quartered
1 pound spinach
1 large plus 3 medium-size yellow onions
Small bunch scallions (optional)
3 large cloves garlic
Small bunch parsley (optional)
Small bunch dill

2 large lemons, plus 1 lemon for garnish (optional)
5 cups chicken stock, preferably homemade (see page 9), or canned
1 stick unsalted butter
1-pint container plain yogurt
1½ cups fruity olive oil
1 cup long-grain white rice
10-ounce box currants
2¼-ounce package shelled pistachio nuts
2 teaspoons cinnamon
Salt
Freshly ground black pepper
1 tablespoon coarsely ground black pepper

UTENSILS

Food processor (optional)
Blender
Broiler pan with rack
Small baking sheet
13 x 9 x 2-inch glass or ceramic dish
Medium-size saucepan
Small heavy-gauge saucepan with cover
Small bowl
Salad spinner (optional)

Measuring cups and spoons
Chef's knife
Paring knife
2 wooden spoons
Ladle
Rubber spatula
Metal tongs
Citrus juicer (optional)
Kitchen scissors (optional)

START-TO-FINISH STEPS

1. Follow chicken recipe steps 1 through 9.
2. While chicken is marinating, follow pilaf recipe steps 1 through 9.
3. While pilaf simmers, follow chicken recipe step 10 and soup recipe steps 1 through 7.
4. Follow chicken recipe step 11.
5. While chicken is broiling, follow pilaf recipe steps 10 through 14.
6. Follow soup recipe step 8 and chicken recipe step 12.
7. While chicken continues to broil and pilaf rests, follow soup recipe step 9 and serve as first course.
8. Follow chicken recipe step 13 and pilaf recipe step 15 and serve.

Spinach Soup with Yogurt

1 pound spinach
2 medium-size yellow onions
4 tablespoons unsalted butter
Small bunch dill
3 cups chicken stock
1½ cups plain yogurt
Salt
Freshly ground black pepper

1. Wash spinach thoroughly in several changes of cold water. Remove and discard tough stems. Dry leaves in salad spinner or with paper towels; set aside.
2. Peel onions and cut enough crosswise into ¼-inch-thick slices to measure 2 cups.
3. Heat butter in medium-size saucepan over medium heat. Add onions and sauté, stirring occasionally, about 2 minutes, or until translucent.
4. Meanwhile, rinse dill and dry with paper towels. Snip enough dill to measure 1 teaspoon; set aside.
5. Increase heat under saucepan to medium-high, add chicken stock, and bring to a boil.
6. Add spinach, stirring and pushing leaves down into stock, and simmer 1 minute.
7. Remove pan from heat and set aside to cool.
8. When cool, combine stock, spinach, onions, and 1 cup yogurt in food processor or blender, and purée.
9. Return soup to saucepan and reheat briefly. Add salt and pepper to taste. Divide soup among 4 bowls, top each serving with a dollop of yogurt, and sprinkle with dill.

Turkish Broiled Chicken

2 large lemons, plus additional lemon for garnish
    (optional)
3 large cloves garlic
1 large yellow onion
2 teaspoons cinnamon
1 teaspoon salt
1 tablespoon coarsely ground black pepper
1½ cups fruity olive oil
2½-pound broiling chicken, quartered
4 sprigs parsley for garnish (optional)

1. Squeeze enough lemon juice to measure ½ cup; set aside.
2. Peel and mince enough garlic to measure 3 tablespoons; set aside.
3. Peel and quarter onion and purée in food processor or blender.
4. Add lemon juice, garlic, cinnamon, salt, and pepper, and process until blended.
5. Turn onion mixture into 13 x 9 x 2-inch glass or ceramic dish. Add olive oil and stir to combine.
6. Rinse chicken and dry with paper towels. Remove and

discard any cartilage or excess fat.
7. Add chicken to marinade and turn to coat. Set aside to marinate at least 15 minutes, turning chicken occasionally.
8. Wash lemon for garnish, if using, and dry with paper towel. Halve lemon and cut one half into quarters; set aside. Reserve remaining half for another use.
9. Wash parsley sprigs, if using, and dry with paper towel; set aside.
10. Preheat broiler.
11. Place chicken, skin-side down, on broiler rack set 6 inches from heating element and broil 10 to 12 minutes.
12. Using tongs, turn chicken and broil other side about 10 minutes, or until juices run clear when chicken is pierced with tip of knife.
13. Transfer chicken to dinner plates and garnish each serving with a lemon wedge and a sprig of parsley, if desired.

Pilaf with Currants and Pistachios

¼ cup currants
¼ cup shelled pistachio nuts
Medium-size yellow onion
4 tablespoons unsalted butter
1 cup long-grain white rice
2 cups chicken stock
Small bunch scallions (optional)

1. Preheat oven to 350 degrees.
2. Place currants in small bowl and add ½ cup warm tap water; set aside to plump.
3. Spread pistachios on small baking sheet and toast in oven, shaking occasionally to prevent scorching, 5 to 7 minutes, or until lightly toasted.
4. Meanwhile, halve and peel onion. Finely chop enough onion to measure ½ cup; set aside. Reserve remaining onion for another use.
5. Remove pistachios from oven and set aside to cool.
6. Heat butter in small heavy-gauge saucepan over medium heat. Add onion and sauté, stirring occasionally, about 2 minutes, or until translucent.
7. Add rice to onion and sauté, stirring, about 3 minutes, or until rice is opaque.
8. Add chicken stock and stir to combine. Increase heat to medium-high and bring to a boil.
9. Cover pan, reduce heat to medium-low, and simmer 15 minutes.
10. Coarsely chop pistachios.
11. Drain currants.
12. Add drained currants and toasted pistachios to rice, and cook another 5 minutes.
13. Meanwhile, if using scallions, wash under cold running water and dry with paper towels. Trim ends and discard. Chop enough scallions to measure ¼ cup; set aside. Reserve remainder for another use.
14. Turn off heat under pan and allow pilaf to rest, covered, at least 10 minutes before serving.
15. To serve, divide pilaf among 4 dinner plates and sprinkle each serving with chopped scallions, if desired.

Garlic and Bread Soup
Pork with Peppers and Onions
Portuguese-style Fried Potatoes

Garlic soup crowned with a poached egg, sautéed pork with roasted peppers, and fried potatoes are a traditional Portuguese meal.

This garlic soup is one of the Portuguese bread-based soups known as *açordas*. In this version, from the province of Minho, the soup is topped with poached eggs and sparked with pungent coriander. When you poach eggs, you cook them in liquid that is barely simmering; this keeps the whites from becoming rubbery. Add the eggs to the poaching liquid one at a time. If desired, you can poach the eggs up to 24 hours in advance. After simmering, put them immediately into a bowl of ice water to stop the cooking process and to keep them moist, then refrigerate. To reheat, dip them briefly in hot water; they will taste just as good in the soup.

WHAT TO DRINK

Dão, a red Portuguese wine, is a fine accompaniment for these dishes, but a California Zinfandel or an Italian Barbera would also be good.

SHOPPING LIST AND STAPLES

Eight ½-inch-thick slices boneless pork loin (about 1½ pounds total weight)
1½ pounds small new red potatoes
2 medium-size yellow onions

1 medium-size yellow bell pepper
2 medium-size red bell peppers
5 large cloves garlic
Large bunch parsley
Small bunch coriander
Large lemon
3 cups chicken stock, preferably homemade (see page 9), or canned
4 eggs
4 tablespoons unsalted butter
1½ cups fruity olive oil
½ teaspoon white wine vinegar
Small baguette
3 tablespoons sugar
1 teaspoon dried thyme
½ teaspoon ground coriander
2 bay leaves
Salt
Freshly ground black pepper
3 whole black peppercorns

UTENSILS

Large heavy-gauge skillet
Medium-size skillet or egg poacher
Large sauté pan
Small saucepan
13 x 9 x 2-inch glass or ceramic baking dish
2 platters, 1 heatproof
Small bowl, plus additional small bowl (if not using mortar and pestle)
Measuring cups and spoons
Chef's knife
Serrated bread knife (optional)
Paring knife
Wooden spoon
Slotted spoon
Ladle
Metal spatula
Long-handled two-pronged fork
Metal tongs
Stiff-bristled brush
Meat pounder or rolling pin
Citrus juicer (optional)
Mortar and pestle (optional)
Brown paper bag

START-TO-FINISH STEPS

One hour ahead: Set out eggs to come to room temperature for soup recipe.

1. Wash parsley and coriander and pat dry with paper towels. Trim stems and discard. Finely chop enough parsley to measure ¼ cup for soup recipe, 2 tablespoons for pork recipe, and 1 teaspoon for potatoes recipe if desired. Finely chop enough coriander to measure ¼ cup for soup recipe. Reserve remaining herbs for another use. Crush garlic cloves under flat blade of chef's knife. Remove peels

and discard. Set aside 1 whole clove for soup recipe. Mince enough remaining garlic to measure 2 tablespoons for soup recipe and 2 tablespoons for pork recipe.
2. Follow pork recipe steps 1 through 8.
3. Follow soup recipe steps 1 through 7.
4. Follow potatoes recipe steps 1 and 2.
5. While potatoes are cooking, follow pork recipe steps 9 through 14.
6. Follow potatoes recipe step 3.
7. Follow soup recipe steps 8 through 12 and serve as first course.
8. Follow pork recipe step 15, potatoes recipe step 4, and serve.

RECIPES

Garlic and Bread Soup

Small baguette
½ cup fruity olive oil
1 large clove garlic, peeled, plus 2 tablespoons minced garlic
¼ teaspoon salt
¼ cup finely chopped parsley
¼ cup finely chopped coriander
½ teaspoon white wine vinegar
3 cups chicken stock
4 eggs, at room temperature

1. Cut bread crosswise into eight ½-inch-thick slices; set aside.
2. Heat ¼ cup oil over medium heat in sauté pan large enough to accommodate bread slices in a single layer. Add peeled garlic clove and sauté 1 minute.
3. Meanwhile, line platter with double thickness of paper towels; set aside.
4. Add bread slices to sauté pan and fry 1 to 2 minutes per side, or until golden brown.
5. Using tongs, transfer bread slices to paper-towel-lined platter to drain; set aside.
6. Combine minced garlic and salt in mortar and mash to a fine paste with pestle. Or, combine in small bowl and mash with back of spoon.
7. Divide garlic paste, parsley, and coriander among 4 soup bowls. Add 1 tablespoon olive oil to each bowl and stir to combine; set aside.
8. Bring 1 quart water and ½ teaspoon white wine vinegar barely to a simmer in medium-size skillet over medium-low heat. Or, bring water to a simmer in egg poacher.
9. Meanwhile, in small saucepan, heat chicken stock over medium-low heat until hot.
10. One by one, crack eggs into a small cup, then slide gently into simmering water. Or, if using egg poacher, crack eggs and slide into poacher cups. Poach eggs 3 minutes.
11. Meanwhile, divide toasted bread slices among soup bowls.
12. Using slotted spoon, place poached eggs on top of bread. Ladle hot stock into bowls and serve immediately.

Pork with Peppers and Onions

Marinade:
3 tablespoons sugar
1 tablespoon salt
3 whole black peppercorns
2 bay leaves
1 teaspoon dried thyme
½ teaspoon ground coriander

Eight ½-inch-thick slices boneless pork loin (about 1½ pounds total weight)
1 medium-size yellow bell pepper
2 medium-size red bell peppers
2 medium-size yellow onions
Large lemon
¾ cup fruity olive oil
1 to 2 tablespoons minced garlic
Salt
Freshly ground black pepper
2 tablespoons finely chopped parsley

1. For marinade, combine sugar, salt, and 2 tablespoons warm tap water in small bowl and stir until dissolved.
2. Under flat blade of chef's knife, bruise peppercorns.
3. Add crushed peppercorns, bay leaves, thyme, coriander, and 1 cup warm water to bowl, and stir to combine; set aside.
4. Trim excess fat from pork and discard. Arrange pork slices in a single layer in 13 x 9 x 2-inch glass or ceramic baking dish.
5. Pour marinade over pork, making sure that marinade covers meat. If not, add a bit more warm water. Set aside to marinate at least 15 minutes.
6. One by one, pierce bell peppers through top with long-handled two-pronged fork and hold directly over gas flame, turning to char skins evenly. Or, place on broiler rack set 3 inches from heating element and broil, turning peppers to char skins evenly. Transfer peppers to brown paper bag, close bag, and set peppers aside to steam.
7. Meanwhile, peel onions and cut enough into ¼-inch-thick slices to measure 2 cups; set aside.
8. Halve lemon and squeeze enough juice to measure ¼ cup; set aside.
9. Preheat oven to 200 degrees.
10. When peppers are cool enough to handle, hold under cold running water and rub gently to remove skins; pat dry with paper towels. Halve and core peppers. Cut peppers lengthwise into ½-inch-wide strips and arrange in single layer on shallow platter. Drizzle with ½ cup olive oil and set aside at room temperature.
11. Meanwhile, heat 2 tablespoons olive oil in large sauté pan over medium heat. Add onions and garlic and sauté, stirring occasionally, 2 minutes, or until translucent but not soft. Add onions and garlic to roasted peppers, season with salt and pepper to taste, and sprinkle with 2 tablespoons lemon juice; toss and set aside.
12. Drain marinade from pork and pat meat dry with paper towels. Place each slice between 2 sheets of waxed paper and pound to ¼-inch thickness with meat pounder or rolling pin. Sprinkle pork with salt and pepper.
13. Add 2 tablespoons olive oil to sauté pan and heat over medium-high heat. Add pork slices and sauté 2 to 3 minutes per side, or until golden brown.
14. Add peppers and onions to pan and sprinkle with remaining lemon juice. Cook 1 to 2 minutes, or just until peppers are heated through. Transfer pork and vegetables to heatproof platter, cover loosely with foil, and keep warm in oven until ready to serve.
15. To serve, divide pork slices among 4 dinner plates, top with equal portions of vegetables, and sprinkle with some chopped parsley.

Portuguese-style Fried Potatoes

1½ pounds small new red potatoes
4 tablespoons unsalted butter
4 tablespoons fruity olive oil
Salt
Freshly ground black pepper
1 teaspoon chopped parsley (optional)

1. Using stiff-bristled brush, scrub potatoes under cold running water, rinse, and dry with paper towels. Do *not* peel. Cut potatoes crosswise into ¼-inch-thick slices; set aside.
2. Combine butter and oil in large heavy-gauge skillet over medium-high heat. When hot, add potatoes and cook, turning occasionally with metal spatula, 15 to 20 minutes, or until potatoes are golden brown and cooked through.
3. Add salt and pepper to taste, cover loosely, and keep warm on stove top until ready to serve.
4. Just before serving, reheat potatoes briefly. Divide potatoes among dinner plates and sprinkle each serving with parsley, if desired.

ADDED TOUCH

A perfectly ripe pineapple is needed for this light dessert. Select a heavy one with a golden rind and deep-green crown leaves.

Pineapple with Port

1½- to 2-pound pineapple
½ cup sugar, approximately
¼ to ½ cup tawny port

1. Trim crown and stem end from pineapple and cut pineapple lengthwise into quarters. Remove core from each quarter and discard. Trim rind and remove any remaining eyes with paring knife. Cut each quarter crosswise into 1-inch chunks and place in large glass bowl.
2. Sprinkle pineapple with sugar to taste, and toss to coat.
3. Sprinkle with port and toss again.
4. Cover bowl with plastic wrap and refrigerate at least 1 hour before serving.

Dennis Gilbert

MENU 1 (Right)
Roasted Baby Chickens with
Sausage and Vegetables
Saffron Rice
Chicory Salad

MENU 2
Cod Basque-Style
Menestra de Legumbres

MENU 3
Fried Haddock Steaks with Sofrito
Escarole Salad with Tomatoes,
Olives, and Anchovies

D ennis Gilbert is a man who cooks for the love of it. He believes that "recipes are only guidelines and that the best meals come from experimenting with the freshest ingredients at hand." Here he prepares three Spanish dinners using traditional cooking techniques but adapting the dishes to foods available in American markets.

Central Spain, famed as "the land of roasting," provides the inspiration for Menu 1, in which baby chickens are quickly browned in olive oil, then roasted to crisp perfection. The chickens are served with sausage and vegetables and golden saffron rice. The salad of sautéed chicory garnished with toasted nuts is presented warm.

The cod recipe of Menu 2 uses a typical Basque method of sauce-making called *pil pil*, which involves simmering potatoes in olive oil until their starch breaks down; the softened potatoes then thicken the liquid in which the fish is poached. A mixed-vegetable stew called *menestra de legumbres* (here topped with eggs) accompanies the fish.

In Menu 3, Dennis Gilbert fries haddock steaks by a traditional Andalusian method and serves them on beds of *sofrito*, a popular Spanish savory sauce of lightly fried chopped vegetables. Escarole is tossed with tomatoes, olives, and anchovies for the salad.

Chicken with spicy sausage and braised vegetables accompanied by saffron rice makes a colorful entrée for a festive Spanish evening. The unusual salad is sautéed chicory topped with nuts.

Roasted Baby Chickens with Sausage and Vegetables
Saffron Rice
Chicory Salad

Baby chickens (also known as *poussins*) are sometimes difficult to obtain, so you may substitute two Rock Cornish game hens that weigh about the same as the chickens. These tiny hens are usually sold frozen but are occasionally available fresh. Cook the hens as you would the baby chickens.

WHAT TO DRINK

The flavors of this menu respond best to a full-bodied white wine, such as a California Chardonnay.

SHOPPING LIST AND STAPLES

2 baby chickens (1 to 1½ pounds each)
¾ pound chorizo, or other spicy sausage
1 head Savoy or white cabbage (about 1 pound)
2 medium-size carrots
2 medium-size heads chicory (about 1¾ pounds total weight)
Medium-size red bell pepper
3 medium-size yellow onions
Small bunch scallions (optional)
6 medium-size cloves garlic
Small bunch fresh mint, or 1 teaspoon dried
Medium-size lemon
3½ cups chicken stock, preferably homemade (see page 9), or canned
1 cup good-quality olive oil, approximately
3 tablespoons balsamic or sherry vinegar
1 cup long-grain white rice
4-ounce package slivered blanched almonds
2-ounce jar pine nuts
1 tablespoon sugar
3 dried hot chili peppers, or 1 teaspoon red pepper flakes, approximately
¼ teaspoon saffron threads
Salt and freshly ground pepper
1 cup dry sherry

UTENSILS

Large heavy-gauge skillet with cover
Medium-size heavy-gauge skillet
Small heavy-gauge saucepan with cover
Roasting pan with rack
Heatproof platter

Large nonaluminum bowl
3 small bowls, 1 nonaluminum
Measuring cups and spoons
Chef's knife
Paring knife
2 wooden spoons
Slotted spoon
Basting brush
Metal tongs
Kitchen string

START-TO-FINISH STEPS

1. Crush and peel garlic. Set aside 2 whole cloves for chicken recipe and mince enough remaining garlic to measure 1 tablespoon each for chicken and salad recipes. Halve lemon and squeeze enough juice to measure 2 tablespoons for chicken recipe and 1 tablespoon for rice recipe. Peel onions. Coarsely chop enough onions to measure 2 cups for chicken recipe and finely chop enough remaining onion to measure ½ cup for rice recipe. Trim scallions, if using, for rice recipe and chop coarsely.
2. Follow rice recipe step 1 and chicken recipe steps 1 through 5.
3. While chicken browns, follow salad recipe steps 1 and 2.
4. Follow chicken recipe step 6.
5. Follow salad recipe step 3 and rice recipe steps 2 and 3.
6. While rice cooks, follow chicken recipe steps 7 through 10 and salad recipe steps 4 through 6.
7. Follow rice recipe step 4.
8. Follow chicken recipe steps 11 through 14, salad recipe step 7, rice recipe step 5, and serve.

RECIPES

Roasted Baby Chickens with Sausage and Vegetables

Small bunch fresh mint, or 1 teaspoon dried, crushed
¾ pound chorizo, or other spicy sausage
2 medium-size carrots
1 head Savoy or white cabbage (about 1 pound)
2 baby chickens (1 to 1½ pounds each)
Salt and freshly ground pepper
2 cloves garlic, crushed, plus 1 tablespoon minced garlic

6 tablespoons good-quality olive oil
1 cup dry sherry
2 tablespoons freshly squeezed lemon juice
2 cups coarsely chopped yellow onions
1½ cups chicken stock

1. Preheat oven to 400 degrees.
2. Wash and dry fresh mint, if using. Reserve 4 sprigs for garnish and mince enough remaining mint to measure 1 tablespoon. Cut sausage into 1-inch pieces.
3. Wash, peel, and trim carrots and halve crosswise. Wash and dry cabbage. Discard any wilted outer leaves and cut cabbage through stem end into 8 wedges; set aside.
4. Sprinkle cavities of chickens with salt and pepper. Place 1 crushed garlic clove and a pinch of fresh or dried mint in each chicken. Using kitchen string, truss each chicken so legs and wings are held close to body.
5. Heat 3 tablespoons olive oil in large heavy-gauge skillet over medium-high heat until it just begins to smoke. Add chickens and sauté, turning with tongs, about 5 to 7 minutes, or until browned on all sides.
6. Place chickens, breast-side up, on rack in roasting pan. Add ½ cup sherry and lemon juice to skillet, increase heat to high, and boil 1 minute, or until reduced slightly. Brush chickens all over with mixture. Pour basting mixture into small bowl and wash and dry skillet. Roast chickens 45 minutes, basting occasionally.
7. Heat remaining 3 tablespoons olive oil in large heavy-gauge skillet over medium heat until hot. Add chopped onions and minced garlic and cook 2 minutes, or until onions are translucent.
8. Add sausage and cook 3 to 5 minutes, or until browned.
9. Add stock, remaining ½ cup sherry, and remaining fresh or dried mint. Increase heat to high and bring mixture to a boil.
10. Add carrots and cabbage, lower heat to medium-low, and simmer, covered, 15 to 20 minutes, or until vegetables are tender.
11. When chickens are done, turn off oven and allow chickens to rest in oven with door ajar.
12. With slotted spoon, transfer cabbage, carrots, and sausage to heatproof platter and keep warm on stove top. Skim fat from cooking liquid and degrease liquid further by blotting surface with paper towels. Boil liquid over high heat 6 to 7 minutes, or until reduced by half.
13. Meanwhile, halve chickens by splitting breast bones with sharp knife, then turning chickens over and splitting backbones. Remove and discard garlic cloves.
14. Arrange chicken halves, sausage, and vegetables on 4 dinner plates. Garnish with mint sprigs, if desired. Serve reduced braising liquid on the side.

Saffron Rice

¼ teaspoon saffron threads
1 tablespoon freshly squeezed lemon juice
1 to 2 tablespoons good-quality olive oil
½ cup finely chopped yellow onion
1 cup long-grain white rice

1 teaspoon salt
2 cups chicken stock
2 small scallions, coarsely chopped (optional)

1. Crumble saffron into small nonaluminum bowl. Add lemon juice and let mixture stand at least 10 minutes.
2. Heat oil in small heavy-gauge saucepan over medium-high heat until hot. Add chopped onion and sauté 2 to 3 minutes, or just until translucent. Add rice and stir to coat grains with oil. Cook rice 2 to 3 minutes, or until golden.
3. Add saffron and lemon juice, salt, and stock; increase heat to high, and bring mixture to a boil. Cover pan, reduce heat to low, and cook 15 to 20 minutes, or until rice is tender.
4. When rice is cooked, remove pan from heat and keep warm on stove top until ready to serve.
5. Just before serving, fluff rice with fork, add chopped scallions, if desired, and divide rice among 4 dinner plates.

Chicory Salad

2 medium-size heads chicory (about 1¾ pounds total weight)
Medium-size red bell pepper
3 dried hot chili peppers, or ½ to 1 teaspoon red pepper flakes
⅓ cup plus 1 tablespoon good-quality olive oil
3 tablespoons balsamic or sherry vinegar
1 tablespoon sugar
1 tablespoon minced garlic
¼ cup slivered blanched almonds
¼ cup pine nuts

1. Wash and dry chicory. Discard any bruised or discolored leaves. Separate outer green leaves from white hearts and cut hearts lengthwise into quarters; set aside hearts and outer leaves. Wash and dry bell pepper. Core, halve, and derib pepper and cut into ¼-inch-wide strips; set aside. If using chili peppers, crush under flat blade of chef's knife, and remove seeds, if desired; set aside.
2. Combine ⅓ cup olive oil, vinegar, sugar, garlic, and crushed peppers or pepper flakes in large nonaluminum bowl and beat with fork until sugar dissolves. Add chicory hearts and toss to coat with marinade. Set aside to marinate at least 20 minutes at room temperature.
3. Heat dry medium-size heavy-gauge skillet over medium heat until hot. Add almonds and pine nuts and toast, shaking pan occasionally, 5 minutes, or until light brown. Transfer nuts to small bowl and set aside.
4. Heat remaining tablespoon olive oil in same medium-size skillet over medium-low heat until hot. Add bell pepper strips and cook 2 minutes, or until soft.
5. Using slotted spoon, add chicory hearts to skillet, reserving marinade. Cook chicory hearts 3 to 4 minutes, or until warm and slightly softened but still crunchy.
6. Add marinade and outer green chicory leaves, toss quickly, and remove pan from heat; set aside.
7. Just before serving, transfer chicory, pepper strips, and marinade to salad bowl and sprinkle with toasted nuts.

Cod Basque-Style
Menestra de Legumbres

For an informal dinner or Sunday brunch, offer fresh cod fillets in a thick sauce and a skillet of vegetable stew.

The mixed vegetable stew calls for broad (or fava) beans, which resemble large lima beans. During the spring, look for fresh broad beans in pods in Middle Eastern or Italian markets and in some supermarkets; broad beans are also sold frozen all year round in many supermarkets. To prepare fresh broad beans, remove them from their pods and wash the beans thoroughly to remove any fuzz.

WHAT TO DRINK

A white wine with acidity and assertiveness would go well with this menu. A California Sauvignon is an excellent first choice, with a French Pouilly-Fumé or Sancerre a fine alternative. Or, try a lightly chilled young red wine, such as a French Beaujolais or a California Gamay.

SHOPPING LIST AND STAPLES

¼ pound lean smoked ham
Four ½- to 1-inch-thick cod fillets (about 2 pounds total weight)
4 all-purpose potatoes (about 1 pound total weight)
2 pounds fresh Italian broad beans, or 10-ounce package frozen
2 pounds fresh peas, or 10-ounce package frozen
Small green bell pepper
Small yellow onion
3 medium-size cloves garlic
Small bunch scallions
Small bunch parsley
4 eggs
1½ cups chicken stock, preferably homemade (see page 9), or canned
1½ cups fish stock, or two 8-ounce bottles clam juice
14-ounce can artichoke hearts
4-ounce jar chopped pimientos
½ cup good-quality olive oil
2 tablespoons all-purpose flour
Salt and freshly ground black pepper

UTENSILS

Stockpot
Large heavy-gauge skillet with cover
12-inch skillet with cover
Small saucepan
Colander
Small strainer
Measuring cups and spoons
Chef's knife
Paring knife
2 wooden spoons
Slotted spatula
Whisk
Vegetable peeler

START-TO-FINISH STEPS

One hour ahead: Set out eggs to come to room temperature for menestra recipe.

1. Wash, dry, and peel potatoes. Halve 1 potato lengthwise and cut into paper-thin slices for cod recipe. Cut 3 potatoes into ½-inch dice for menestra recipe. Peel garlic; mince 1 clove for cod recipe and 2 cloves for menestra recipe.
2. Follow cod recipe steps 1 and 2.
3. While potatoes cook, follow menestra recipe steps 1 through 5.
4. Follow cod recipe step 3.
5. While cod poaches, follow menestra recipe steps 6 and 7.
6. While eggs cook, follow cod recipe steps 4 through 6.
7. Follow menestra recipe step 8 and serve with cod.

RECIPES

Cod Basque-Style

Four ½- to 1-inch-thick cod fillets (about 2 pounds total weight)
Small bunch parsley
Small yellow onion
¼ cup good-quality olive oil
1 all-purpose potato, peeled and cut into paper-thin slices
1½ cups fish stock or clam juice
1 medium-size clove garlic, minced
Freshly ground black pepper

1. Rinse cod fillets and dry with paper towels. Wash and dry parsley. Coarsely chop enough parsley to measure ⅓ cup. Peel and coarsely chop onion.
2. Heat olive oil in large heavy-gauge skillet over medium heat until hot. Add onion and cook, stirring, 1 minute, or until softened but not browned. Reduce heat to low, add potato slices, and cook, covered, 20 minutes, or until po-

tatoes soften and begin to fall apart.

3. Top potato slices with cod fillets and add stock. Increase heat to medium-high and bring liquid to a simmer. Cover skillet, reduce heat to very low, and poach fish 5 to 7 minutes, or until it flakes easily when pierced with knife.

4. Using slotted spatula, transfer fish to serving platter, cover with foil, and keep warm on stove top.

5. Increase heat under skillet to high and boil cooking liquid, whisking occasionally, 6 to 7 minutes, or until it is reduced by half.

6. Remove skillet from heat, add minced garlic, parsley, and pepper to taste, and whisk until combined. Spoon sauce over fish and serve.

Menestra de Legumbres

Salt
2 pounds fresh Italian broad beans, or 10-ounce package frozen
2 pounds fresh peas, or 10-ounce package frozen
14-ounce can artichoke hearts
4-ounce jar chopped pimientos
¼ c - Small green bell pepper
1 scallion
¼ pound lean smoked ham
¼ cup good-quality olive oil
3 all-purpose potatoes, peeled and cut into ½-inch dice
2 medium-size cloves garlic, minced
2 tablespoons all-purpose flour
1½ cups chicken stock
4 eggs, at room temperature

1. In stockpot, bring 2 quarts water and 1 teaspoon salt to a boil. Meanwhile, shell enough fresh beans and peas, if using, to measure 2 cups each; set aside.

2. Drain artichoke hearts in colander; transfer to small bowl. Drain pimientos in small strainer; set aside.

3. Wash and dry bell pepper. Core and seed pepper and mince enough to measure ¼ cup. Wash, trim, and mince scallion. Dice ham.

4. Add fresh broad beans and fresh peas to stockpot of boiling water and blanch 1 to 2 minutes, or until vegetables become bright in color. If using frozen vegetables, cook, following package directions, just until thawed. Turn vegetables into colander and refresh under cold water.

5. Heat 2 tablespoons olive oil in 12-inch skillet over medium-high heat until oil just begins to smoke. Add diced potatoes and stir to coat with oil. Reduce heat to medium

and cook potatoes, stirring constantly, 5 minutes, or until well browned. Add diced ham and cook, stirring, another 5 minutes, or until ham is browned. Remove pan from heat, cover, and keep warm on stove top.

6. Heat remaining 2 tablespoons oil in small saucepan over medium heat until hot. Add minced garlic, bell pepper, and scallions and cook 2 minutes, or until softened. Stir in flour and cook another minute. Add stock, increase heat to medium-high, and bring sauce to a boil. Remove sauce from heat; set aside.

7. Add broad beans, peas, artichoke hearts, and pimientos to skillet with potatoes and ham and warm over low heat. Add sauce and stir to combine. Break eggs into skillet, cover tightly, and cook 10 to 12 minutes, or until eggs are of desired firmness.

8. Serve menestra directly from skillet.

ADDED TOUCH

If the soup seems too thick, add more stock.

Garlic and Almond Soup

6 large cloves garlic
3 small scallions
1 cup blanched, toasted almonds
¼ cup good-quality olive oil
6 slices French or Italian bread, each 1 inch thick
1 teaspoon dried thyme
½ teaspoon fennel seeds
2 cups chicken stock, approximately
¼ cup dry sherry
1 to 2 teaspoons minced parsley
Freshly ground pepper

1. Peel and mince garlic. Wash, dry, and chop scallions.

2. In large skillet, heat 2 tablespoons olive oil over medium heat until hot but not smoking. Add bread slices and fry 1 minute, or until golden brown. Add remaining 2 tablespoons oil, turn slices, and fry another minute.

3. Place almonds, fried bread, minced garlic, chopped scallions, thyme, fennel seeds, 2 cups stock, 2 cups water, and sherry in large heavy-gauge saucepan and stir to combine. Bring liquid to a boil over medium-high heat. Skim fat and simmer soup 20 minutes.

4. Remove soup from heat and allow to cool slightly. When cooled, purée soup in blender or food processor. Transfer soup to tureen and stir in parsley and pepper to taste.

Fried Haddock Steaks with Sofrito
Escarole Salad with Tomatoes, Olives, and Anchovies

Fried haddock steaks garnished with watercress, olives, and pimiento strips rest on a sauce of chopped vegetables flavored with smoked ham. Refresh the palate with a light tossed salad and, if desired, serve bread to dip into the sauce.

I f you do not care for haddock, select any other firm-fleshed white fish for this meal. Purchase either four small whole fish or four fish steaks; fillets should be used only if the fish is extremely fresh and firm.

The faintly bitter flavor of escarole (also known as Batavian endive) goes well with the fish. Escarole has a bushy head of broad leaves that curl slightly at the tips. Select a head that has fresh-looking, crisp leaves with good color on the outer edges, and use it as soon as possible. If you must store escarole, place it unwashed in a plastic bag in the refrigerator. Before using, wash the leaves thoroughly but quickly under cold running water; soaking leaches their flavor.

WHAT TO DRINK

A crisp well-chilled white wine is called for here. Try a Portuguese Vinho Verde, an Italian Verdicchio, or a French Muscadet.

SHOPPING LIST AND STAPLES

¼ pound lean smoked ham
Four 1¼-inch-thick haddock steaks, with bone (about 2 pounds total weight)
Large green bell pepper
Small red bell pepper
Medium-size head escarole
2 medium-size tomatoes
2 medium-size yellow onions
Small bunch scallions
2 small cloves garlic
Small bunch parsley
Small bunch watercress (optional)
Medium-size lemon
Medium-size juice orange
2-ounce jar pimientos (optional)
3½-ounce can pitted black olives (optional)
5¾-ounce jar pitted brine-cured green olives
2-ounce tin anchovy fillets
½ cup plus 2 tablespoons virgin olive oil, approximately
⅓ cup extra-virgin olive oil
4-ounce bottle aromatic bitters
⅓ cup all-purpose flour
1½ tablespoons paprika
Salt and freshly ground black pepper
¼ cup dry sherry

UTENSILS

Food processor or blender
2 large heavy-gauge skillets, 1 with cover
Salad bowl
Large bowl
Small nonaluminum bowl
Salad spinner (optional)
Small strainer
Measuring cups and spoons
Chef's knife
Paring knife
2 wooden spoons
Slotted spatula

START-TO-FINISH STEPS

1. Prepare pimiento, olives, and watercress, if using, for haddock recipe; set aside. Crush and peel garlic. Mince enough garlic to measure 1 teaspoon each for haddock and salad recipes; set aside.
2. Follow haddock recipe steps 1 through 4.
3. While sofrito is cooking, follow salad recipe steps 1 through 5.
4. Follow haddock recipe steps 5 and 6.
5. Follow salad recipe step 6, haddock recipe step 7, and serve.

RECIPES

Fried Haddock Steaks with Sofrito

Small bunch parsley
Large green bell pepper
Small red bell pepper
2 medium-size yellow onions
¼ pound lean smoked ham
½ cup plus 2 tablespoons virgin olive oil, approximately
¼ cup dry sherry
1½ tablespoons paprika
Freshly ground black pepper
Four 1¼-inch-thick haddock steaks, with bone (about
    2 pounds total weight)
⅓ cup all-purpose flour
1 teaspoon minced garlic
1 pimiento, cut into strips (optional)
¼ cup pitted black olives, drained (optional)
4 sprigs watercress (optional)

1. Wash and dry parsley; trim stems and discard. Mince enough parsley to measure ¼ cup. Wash and dry bell peppers. Core, seed, and quarter peppers. Halve, peel, and quarter onions. Finely chop enough ham to measure about ⅔ cup.
2. Combine onions and bell peppers in food processor or blender and process until finely chopped.
3. Heat 2 tablespoons olive oil in large heavy-gauge skillet over medium heat until hot. Add onions and peppers and cook 2 to 3 minutes, or until vegetables are softened. Add

ham and cook another 3 minutes, or until ham just begins to brown.
4. Stir in minced parsley, sherry, ⅓ cup water, paprika, and pepper to taste. Bring sofrito to a simmer, and cook over low heat, partially covered, 20 minutes, or until ingredients have softened to a marmalade consistency.
5. When sofrito is cooked, remove from heat and keep warm on stove top. Rinse haddock steaks and dry with paper towels. Place flour on sheet of waxed paper. Line platter with double thickness of paper towels.
6. Pour enough olive oil into large heavy-gauge skillet to come to a depth of ¼ inch. Heat oil over medium-high heat until hot but not smoking. Dredge haddock steaks in flour, shaking off excess. Carefully place haddock steaks into skillet and fry, turning several times, 10 to 15 minutes, or until flesh is browned and flakes easily when pierced with tip of knife. Using slotted spatula, transfer haddock steaks to paper-towel-lined platter to drain briefly.
7. To serve, stir minced garlic into sofrito and divide sofrito among 4 dinner plates. Arrange haddock steaks on top of sofrito and garnish each steak with a pimiento strip, an olive, and a sprig of watercress, if desired.

Escarole Salad with Tomatoes, Olives, and Anchovies

2-ounce tin anchovy fillets
1 cup pitted brine-cured green olives
Medium-size head escarole
Medium-size lemon
Medium-size juice orange
⅓ cup extra-virgin olive oil
2 teaspoons aromatic bitters
1 teaspoon minced garlic
Salt
Freshly ground black pepper
3 medium-size scallions
2 medium-size tomatoes

1. Rinse anchovies in small strainer and pat dry with paper towels. Drain olives; set aside.
2. Separate escarole leaves, discarding any that are bruised or discolored. Wash leaves well and dry in salad spinner or with paper towels. Tear leaves into small pieces, place in large bowl, cover with plastic wrap, and refrigerate until ready to use.
3. Halve lemon and orange. Squeeze enough lemon juice to measure 2 tablespoons and enough orange juice to measure ⅓ cup.
4. Combine lemon juice, orange juice, olive oil, bitters, garlic, ¼ teaspoon salt, and pepper to taste in small nonaluminum bowl. Blend dressing well with fork.
5. Wash scallions and tomatoes and dry with paper towels. Trim and coarsely chop scallions. Core tomatoes and cut into wedges. Place scallions, olives, and tomatoes in salad bowl, add dressing, and toss to coat well. Set aside at room temperature at least 30 minutes.
6. Just before serving, add escarole leaves, and anchovy fillets to taste, to salad bowl and toss to combine.

Acknowledgments

The Editors would like to thank the following for their courtesy in lending items for photography: *Cover:* plates—ceramic designer Claire Des Becker; fork—Wolfman-Gold & Good Co.; rug—Al Della Fera; underplate—Amigo Country, NYC. *Frontispiece:* tiles—Country Floors; copper basin, jugs, small bowls—Amigo Country; kilim—La Chambre Perse; baskets, box—Be Seated; square plate—Julien Mousa-Oghli; carafe—Pottery Barn. *Pages 16–17:* tiles—Nemo Tile; casserole—Pottery Barn; servers—Gorham; platters, napkins, plates—Frank McIntosh at Henri Bendel. *Pages 20–21:* napkins—Pierre Deux; underplates—Frank McIntosh at Henri Bendel; tablecloth—Laura Ashley; flatware, glasses—Gorham; plates—Ad Hoc Housewares. *Page 23:* napkin, tablecloth—Laura Ashley; plate—Frank McIntosh at Henri Bendel. *Pages 26–27:* plates—Haviland & Co. *Page 30:* tablecloth—Pierre Deux; fork—Gorham; plates—Feu Follet. *Page 33:* plates, tablecloth, napkins—Pierre Deux; pan—Charles Lamalle. *Pages 36–37:* dishes—Ceramica Mia; tiles—Country Floors. *Page 40:* tablecloth—Conran's; fork—Gorham; dinner plate, napkin—Broadway Panhandler, NYC. *Page 43:* tiles—Country Floors; platters, servers—Amigo Country; skewers—Charles Lamalle. *Pages 46–47:* platters, bowl—ceramic designer Claire Des Becker; baskets, copper plate—Be Seated. *Page 50:* mat—Be Seated; plates—Pottery Barn; flatware—Gorham. *Page 52:* platters—ceramic designer Claire Des Becker; runner—Stevie Bass. *Pages 54–55:* glasses, flatware—Gorham; dishes—Chelsea Passage at Barney's; napkins—"Mum" Lindlaw. *Page 58:* plates—Dan Levy courtesy of Creative Resources; napkin—Creative Resources; flatware—Gorham; tabletop—Formica® Brand Laminate by Formica Corp. *Page 61:* tablecloth—Ad Hoc Softwares; flatware—Gorham. *Pages 64–65:* tiles—Country Floors; tray—Feu Follet; glass, flatware—Gorham. *Page 68:* platter—Pierre Deux; pan—Charles Lamalle; tiles—Country Floors. *Page 71:* tiles—Country Floors; bowl—Eigen Arts; white platter—Louis Lourioux; beige tray—Pottery Barn. *Pages 74–75:* rug—Conran's; underplates—Pottery Barn; plates, bowls—Dan Levy; glasses, flatware—Gorham. *Page 78:* plates, platter—Mad Monk; napkin, tablecloth—Stevie Bass. *Page 81:* rug, white platters—City Life. *Pages 84–85:* cataplana pan—Williams Sonoma; salad bowl, thermos, mugs, vase—Wolfman-Gold & Good Co.; napkins, blue bowl—Broadway Panhandler, NYC. *Pages 88–89:* rug—Al Della Fera; flatware, glasses—Gorham; pitcher—Young Collection. *Page 91:* underplate—City Life; plate—Japan Interiors Gallery; flatware—Camilla Toniola and Eric Beason. *Pages 94–95:* plates—Eigen Arts; flatware—Gorham. *Page 98:* tiles—Nemo Tile; trays—Be Seated. *Page 101:* plates, bowls—Bowl & Board; napkin—Leacock & Co.

Illustrations by Ray Skibinski

Production by Giga Communications

Index

Time-Life Books Inc. offers a wide range of fine recordings, including a Big Band series. For subscription information, call 1-800-621-7026, or write TIME-LIFE MUSIC, *Time & Life Building, Chicago, Illinois 60611.*